ELLIE BUS

THE
Realistic
OPTIMIST

A *Collection* OF ESSAYS

outskirts
press

Acknowledgements

The essays in this book were previously published in The Other Paper, South Burlington, Vermont, as a monthly column, titled, The Realistic Optimist. I am extremely grateful to the previous Publisher and Editor, Judy Kearns, for inviting me to write a regular column and also the freedom to republish the columns.

A big huge thank you goes to those readers of my columns who encouraged and inspired me to consider publishing a collection of them in a book.

My loving family has been, and continues to be, a fountain of encouragement, inspiration, assistance, humor and support. I feel a deep sense of gratitude for the various ways my husband and three sons have contributed to the birth of this book. My oldest son, John, took the beautiful photo on the cover during a trip to Victoria, British Columbia. My husband, Hack, modified and edited the photo for the book cover and did so much more. Kevin wrote the wonderful Foreword. Scott read the developing plans and essays for the book and made helpful comments.

I also want to thank all the staff at Outskirts Press who did so much to bring this book into a lovely finished reality. Many thanks especially to Allison Hiles, who was my initial contact. Also, Elaine Simpson, who answered my every question or concern and guided me through the entire production process to the finished product and beyond.

Foreword

Going back as far as I can remember, my mother was always a realistic optimist.

When she was asked in 2009 to write a monthly column for *The Other Paper* in South Burlington, Vermont, she gave me a call and we brainstormed for a bit. Finally, I said: Why don't you call it The Realistic Optimist?

That title, in so many ways, embodied her signature perspective: Pursue your dreams with energy and passion, stick closely to your ideals, but do so in a way that is both realistic and meaningful.

As a young boy growing up near Worcester, Mass., I saw that perspective in action. My mother worked as a nurse for the Visiting Nurse Association in the city. She cared for children and adults in a rundown, public housing project. She worked with children who had been physically and emotionally abused, mothers and fathers who were physically abusive with each other, and drug addicts who were struggling with parenting their children.

Based on the conversations she had with fellow nurses and my father, that I sometimes eavesdropped on, she did not believe she was going to transform the lives of the people in the public housing project in some wildly optimistic way. What she did believe is that what she was doing did make their lives better.

Starting with her inaugural column, on May 28, 2009, I witnessed that perspective as a reader. That first column was about a very persistent squirrel in her backyard that lived by the motto: If at first you don't succeed, try, try again. Basically, the squirrel, which she nicknamed Flip, was trying to get food out of a squirrel-proof bird feeder. He was relentless as described in the essay, Backyard Life Lessons.

Such lessons clearly resonated with readers. One day, I had stopped to take a rest on a bike path in South Burlington after a relatively long rollerblading outing. I was sitting on the ground, when an older gentleman, wearing a baseball cap, walked over to inquire if I was OK. We got talking and I introduced myself.

He asked: Your last name is Bushweller? Are you related to Ellie Bushweller, that woman who writes for The Other Paper?

Yup, that's my Mom.

Well, then please tell her I always read her column

On another occasion, a family friend talking about how much he enjoyed her most recent column, told me he looks for her column first when he gets the paper.

It does not surprise me that readers loved her columns. She comes from a long line of Irish American storytellers, she has lived in many places, raised three sons, and now has eight grandchildren. She has experienced the thrill of victory and the agony of defeat in the game of life, and she brings that perspective to her writing.

A big part of my mother's realistic optimism is about embracing the journey rather than getting bogged down by an obsession with the destination. She's not afraid to try new things That's why she laughed at herself when she was struggling to learn how to text, why she was a keen observer of human behavior while stranded in an airport, as she describes in Airline Purgatory, and why that squirrel, Flip, will always symbolize the spirit of the Realistic Optimist.

Kevin Bushweller

Table of Contents

Animal
Antics

Backyard Life Lessons

The teacher was quite small in stature with beady black eyes. One thing I noticed immediately was that he was unusually athletic. The sunny spring day he first arrived to become my life coach, he back flipped his way across our backyard to a large maple tree at the opposite end. He was the most playful, amusing squirrel I had ever seen. However, when he had a task, he set about it with total focus, unrelenting determination, and a heavy dose of patience that truly amazed me.

I named this furry visiting professor, Flip, for obvious reasons. Through the years, I have had many memorable teachers, but none taught me more about life than Flip. He was a constant visitor to our backyard for over three years, probably because we provided a number of challenging supermarkets.

I loved having a variety of birds visiting our yard so there were multiple birdfeeders everywhere. These were Flip's most effective teaching tools. All squirrels have one obvious principle which guides their every action: Success is Not Accepting Failure. They never give up even when the odds seem totally stacked against them.

And so the bell, in the backyard school room, rang one early morning and classes began for this unsuspecting student gazing out the sunroom window. The label on the green metal birdfeeder, hanging from one of our maple trees, read: Totally Squirrel Proof. Yellow stickers with black lettering on the sides of the feeder confidently stated Squirrels, no free lunch. Flip jumped past the sticker and on to the feeding bar. I can't tell you how many times over the next two weeks, Flip landed on the bar only to have it close the opening to the birdseed. The bar was set up to close when a certain weight was on it. It almost proved to be truly squirrel proof.

However, after multiple failed attempts on the bar, Flip developed a new strategy. He hung upside down, on the side of the feeder, and touched the bar lightly with one paw, releasing a cascade of seed out the side. Bingo!

How often in life do we tend to give up too soon or keep trying the same old approach to a problem for too long when it obviously doesn't work? Flip decided to try another way to overcome a seemingly insurmountable obstacle and finally succeeded.

There is a framed photo of Flip in my study. He is upside down on a birdfeeder. As he happily munches away on the birdseed, there is a sign just above his head, Squirrels, no free lunch.

Honor Guard

For years, a tall, full leafed maple tree stood in our back-yard. Several birdfeeders and a birdhouse hung from its strong, outstretched limbs. Each spring, a pair of small birds would build their nest and raise their young in that birdhouse. Looking out the windows and watching all the activity through every season was a favorite pastime.

The maple tree survived the ice storm of 1998 but suffered irreversible damage as the result of a drought that lasted almost a year. We noticed the leaves were smaller and fell much earlier in the fall. Then came the spring when no leaves appeared on the top branches at all. We called in a tree doctor. He did not have good news. However, he did suggest some remedies we could try to save the dying tree. The damage proved too pervasive. I remember the day I stood sadly by the tree with my back pressed up against it, knowing the time had come to have it taken down.

The tree surgeons arrived early one fall morning and rang our bell. My husband told them where they could find the tree in the yard. It was only moments later when the doorbell rang again. One of the three men told us, in a very excited tone, there was a large Barred Owl in the tree. He asked would we like to come and see it and bring a camera. These three grown men were as awestruck as we were looking at this majestic bird. We never had any type of owl visit our yard. The owl sat in regal splendor, his eyes taking us in while we were gazing back at him. You could hear the click, click of my husband's camera. The owl did not move a feather!

Finally, one of the men picked up a chain saw and turned it on in hopes the bird would leave the tree. They did not want to harm this beautiful creature. The owl, in slight annoyance, moved from the tree to the limb of a nearby tree. He remained there during the noisy process of taking the tree down including sawing the limbs and trunk into smaller pieces. The owl sat motionless staring at the tree the whole time. He did not flinch once. There he remained sitting on the limb all afternoon. It was a fascinating sight. You couldn't help but feel a certain yet strange symbolism as this scene played out. Had the regal owl come to pay homage to a fallen friend of the forest?

Eventually, the job was completed. The men left. Each worker left with a picture of the owl in hand. Our cherished tree was now just a memory as the afternoon sun began to set. Only the stump of the tree remained. Our visitor, the owl, swooped down and stood on the stump for a while before taking flight, never to return to our yard again.

A Most Unusual Pair

From the time I was a young child, I was always surrounded by pets. There was usually a dog and cat in our home, and a variety of fish and turtles. After I was married and had children, at one point, we added one or two pet rabbits to the mix. I love animals and enjoy watching some of their funny antics when at play. Friends will often send me cartoons, jokes or videos of animals doing the craziest things.

However, recently, a friend sent me the most touching video telling the story of the survival of a small kitten. An older couple was sitting on their porch when they saw a kitten come bouncing across their yard, followed by a large black crow. The crow appeared to have assumed the role of surrogate mother to this young kitten. The crow would pick up food in its beak and place the food in the mouth of the kitten periodically. Sometimes the kitten would romp around the yard with the crow hopping quickly beside it and they would roll together briefly. There was never a sign of aggression at any time for this most unusual pair. What an amazing sight.

The older couple eventually called their vet to discuss this situation with her. The vet recommended the couple video tape the scene to truly verify the unique relationship this crow had established with this kitten. It became obvious the kitten had been abandoned and would not have survived had the crow not taken on the nurturing mother role.

Eventually, the couple took in the kitten to live with them. However, the crow continued to remain involved with the kitten. Each day at a certain time, it would peck on a window and the couple would let the growing kitten out to be with the crow. Even as the kitten began to grow into a full grown cat, this very unusual pair remained friends. Nature had originally assigned them the role of mortal enemies but the needs of a helpless kitten had made them friends for life.

Animals play an important role in our lives. They give love unconditionally and are so forgiving and only ask the same from us. They have a lot to teach us about life.

The Stowaway

Have you ever had one of those lazy, hazy days when you are lost in thought, going about your routine tasks for the day? Then suddenly something totally unexpected jolts you back to reality in an instant?

This past August, my husband and I were spending two relaxing two weeks in a cabin, by a lovely lake, located in a wooded area in New Hampshire. Each morning, I enjoyed driving the ten miles to a small local grocery store to pick up the newspaper, and some yummy muffins for breakfast and chat with the people in the store.

One sunny morning, I parked the car and went to get the paper, as usual. When I came out of the store, I was taking in all the colorful scenery around the area, relishing the start of a new day. Thoughts of kayaking later that day were dancing happily in my head.

When I got to the car, I opened the back door to place my package on the seat. There on the seat, in the middle of the car, sat a very healthy, brown adult field mouse, with beady black eyes, staring back at me. For a few moments, we both just stared at each other in total shock and utter surprise! Then I let out a few expletives and the mouse jumped from the back seat and ran under the front seat, disappearing from view.

Having grown up in Brooklyn, New York, I felt like the city girl meets the country mouse, but a little too up close and personal! The only technology we brought with us to the cabin was our cellphones for emergencies. I quickly called my husband to report our stowaway. Then I carefully drove back to the cabin, hoping against hope, the mouse would not get lodged under the gas or brake pedal. The ten miles of winding road seemed endless. I think the mouse was as anxious as I was. She never made an appearance while the car was in motion. Yes, it was a she!

My husband took some wooden planks he had and set up a ramp from the open front door of the car to the ground outside. He asked me to get a jar of peanut butter, knife, plastic container and a flat piece of cardboard. He applied small globs of peanut butter at intervals down the planks. Then, like a patient cat, he waited. It was all accomplished in an instant. The mouse eventually came out to eat the peanut butter. My husband had her in the plastic container and slid the cardboard underneath it within seconds.

That field mouse never knew how very lucky she was. My husband walked into the woods behind the cabin and released her. If he had been unable to capture and release her that way, the next plan was the guillotine, a mouse trap!

Days later, when I was riding in the front seat of the car, I made an amusing discovery. Our little stowaway had found a bag of tissue in a side pocket of the door. The tissue had been neatly shredded and made into a nest in the pocket. She was getting ready to provide us with a whole bunch of newborn stowaways when she was interrupted.

Timing is everything!

Backyard Life Lessons Revisited

A relative of Flip is back! Flip was the amazing squirrel I wrote about in my first article for The Other Paper, May 28, 2009. He not only did multiple back flips across our yard, he succeeded in mastering the birdfeeder for his lunch! This green metal feeder had a label on the back: Totally Squirrel Proof and a sticker on both sides which stated: Squirrels No Free Lunch. However, with total focus and lots of determination and patience, he was a powerful teacher in the art of successful problem solving.

The name I have given our latest athlete is Fat Albert. He's not really fat at all, just the most solid, muscular, confident squirrel I have ever seen. He doesn't do back flips. What he does is literally fly at great speed off the base of the feeder. Then he grasps the cage of another squirrel proof feeder.

This accomplishment did not happen overnight. In fact, it took Fat Albert six months to figure out how to master it. This feeder is a long metal pole. It has a round bell shaped attachment three quarters of the way up to prevent squirrels from getting to the four cross bars above that hold four feeders. Fat Albert had his sights set on the feeder containing suet and seed. Every squirrel, who has come to munch on the fallen seed at the bottom of the pole, tried to climb to the top unsuccessfully. Only Fat Albert eventually figured out a strategy, after six months of repeated failures. The pole has been in place for the last five years. Many squirrels have come and gone and never gained access to the feeders at the top.

Every morning when Fat Albert came to the feeders, he would take a running leap on to the pole but eventually fall or slide off. That never discouraged him from trying it repeated times on each visit. Just when we were beginning to think we REALLY did have a squirrel proof feeder, Fat Albert ran as fast as he could up the pole and leaped in the air, spread eagle, to grasp the cage of another birdfeeder. That was about two months ago and he has been doing it successfully every time since then. He leaps on and straddles the crossbar to the suet and seed feeder and gorges himself. My husband and I have tried spraying him with a high powered toy water pistol and even the hose. He looks us straight in the eye and stands his ground on the pole till he is soaked. Then he leaves for a time but always returns to munch again. You can't avoid admiring that kind of steely determination and chutzpah.

Fat Albert, like Flip before him, reminds me repeated failures do not foretell ultimate success. Believe in your ability to solve any problem using all the skills you have at your disposal.

The Kindness of Animals

While waiting in a doctor's office recently, the title of an article, on the front cover of a magazine, caught my eye, Therapy Cats. I had read other stories, in the past, about the work of therapy dogs. In my work as a community nurse in Worcester, Massachusetts years ago, I had even had some experiences caring for patients with seeing eye dogs. However, I had never come across therapy cats.

The article opened up with the story of one cat that had been living in a nursing home for several years. This cat had arrived one morning, at the home, as a young, scraggly kitten. A staff member took it in and fed it. Eventually, the decision was made to keep the kitten at the nursing home. As the kitten grew more mature, the staff began to notice him going from room to room, spending time in the laps of patients or on the bed next to them. It is a fact that petting a cat can help to reduce stress and lower blood pressure. Non responsive patients reached out to pet the cat and the cat purred happily in their presence.

An elderly couple, married more than sixty years lived at this particular nursing home. One year, the wife died, and the husband was actively grieving the loss. He sat in his chair, refusing to eat hardly anything and almost never spoke. A staff member walking past his room one morning saw the cat walk in and jump on the man's lap. The cat sat up on its hind legs and put each paw on one shoulder of the man and just looked straight at him. He stayed like that for several minutes then curled up in the man's lap for the rest of the day. The elderly man reached out and began to pet the cat. Every day the cat would repeat the same ritual with this sad man. Slowly, the staff noticed the mood of the man began to lift.

After reading this touching story, I searched the internet for more information on the work of therapy cats. In most cases, therapy cats do not live at the facility. They are brought by their owners to the nursing homes for visits. Cats used for therapy need to have calm, steady, friendly personalities. They are not only helping in facilities but also with children dealing with autism. The Foundation for Pet Provided Therapy and The Delta Society are two organizations that certify cats as therapy cats.

I have always been an animal lover for as long as I can remember. Growing up, there was always a dog and cat living with us. As a child, I got together with three friends and we formed the Be Kind to Animals Club. We put out an informational newsletter weekly, walking our Brooklyn neighborhood, selling copies for five cents. One year, we wrote a play and put it on to help raise money for the new facility to be built for the humane society. A local radio show picked up this as a human interest story. The commentator reported how these four young girls had managed to provide a few bricks for the new building with their own original play as a neighborhood fundraiser.

Animals can touch our lives in so many positive ways. The use of dogs and cats, and other animals, in providing some much needed unconditional love and kindness to people living in facilities or children with autism is impressive.

*Technology
Tales*

Finding Digital Balance

Graduation speeches are all too soon forgotten, not just by the graduates, but all who attend the ceremony. In honesty, I can't remember any speeches from my own graduations. As a mother of three sons, only one graduation speech lingers in my memory. It was given by my oldest son at his high school graduation. He dedicated it to a good friend who, the previous year, had committed suicide. The poignancy of his words is etched in my memory forever.

This year, I didn't hear any speeches but did read about two talks that really caught my attention. Both talks dealt with how to live with balance in a world full of email, Facebook, You Tube, Twitter and just the Web alone. One that surprised and delighted me the most was given by Eric Schmidt, the CEO of Google, at the University of Pennsylvania on May 18th. On the Google website, his speech was described as: Goggle CEO Shares the Meaning of Life. This was followed by the subtitle: Talks Technology Past, Present and Future. He was amusing as he compared his own college days to the present graduates. Two examples:

- We used 700 dollars VCR'S. You have You Tube.

- We had phone booths. Remember them? You have cellphones.

Although I enjoyed Eric's entire speech and found it, not only amusing but inspirational, the ending was what caught my attention the most. This technology pioneer was suggesting and encouraging these newly minted graduates to turn off your computer and your phone and discover all that is human around us. Eric Schmidt, Google CEO, advising young people heading into the rest of their lives, not to stop enjoying the benefits of all the gadgets, just push the pause button regularly. He understood the importance of carefully observing the world around us directly, with all the senses, and the profound value of face to face interactions.

Locally, a respected University of Vermont professor, Dr. Glen Elder, gave a similar speech at the commencement ceremony for the College of Arts and Sciences. He was also amusing and engaging yet warned the students of the ways in which real life is not like Facebook. That talk was given about a week before Dr. Elder, age 42, collapsed and died of an apparent heart attack while out jogging.

Both men were pursuing totally different careers yet sharing a common theme. I think they were asking the graduates to seek a balance between technology and the world and people around them. Life was never meant to be lived as a spectator sport residing totally in a land of virtual reality.

I began to search the internet for articles on the impact of technology on social isolation. It is amazing how much is written on this specific topic. There is concern out there. These two commencement speakers were right on target.

I decided to take stock of my own involvement with technology.

To my surprise, I was beginning to get a bit obsessive about checking my email numerous times daily and wandering around the internet.

Now, one day weekly, my finger presses the off key and I listen to the dingdong melody as my computer screen goes blank. A strange sense of relief enters my body as the familiar hum of my laptop disappears.

Texting Tales

Thumbs moving across the cellphone keys with lightning speed! I watched in amazement this summer as my teenage grandchildren were texting back and forth. It's so easy, Gram. Try it. I'll teach you. And this late bloomer was born into the wonderful, wacky world of texting. In my case, it's not just thumbs; I'm all fingers in search of the letter I need to complete just one word. Then I wonder, do I sign a text like a letter to family and friends with my usual Love? Watching both the keyboard speed and frequent access of the savvy thumb texting users, I am convinced, one day soon, we will have a new health diagnosis: Carpal Tunnel Thumbs.

I read recently that in London they solved a rapidly increasing texting problem in a rather hilarious way. So many pedestrians were getting injured while walking and texting, they decided to pad the lampposts!

Text messaging is an efficient way to communicate with others. As text message usage explodes, etiquette guidelines are appearing on the scene. As a neophyte, I felt compelled to read several articles on the etiquette of texting. Don't use all capitals! It is the same as yelling at a person. Don't use a text message to end a relationship. Well, why be in a relationship at all, if you can't say what you have to say in person, face to face? Even the great-granddaughter of Emily Post, Cindy Post, has weighed in on texting and family meals: No texting at the dinner table, particularly at home. The family meal is a social event, not a food ingestion event.

Although teenage girls are reported to be the most frequent users of texting, men are a close second. In the current business climate men and women worry about job performance and rapid response. They feel compelled to stay connected to the workplace 24/7 via texting or other technologies. Consequently, they blur the boundaries between work and family. In one case, a family of four sat down to discuss Dad's constant texting at the dinner table. It was young twin girls who took Dad to task. Fortunately, the chagrined father agreed to stop texting during dinner. Oh, the wisdom of children! A father of four shared with me his recent experience about his teenage son's texting gone wild. A jaw dropping cellphone bill arrived revealing his son had racked up 5,000 text messages in one month!

Cellphone use or texting while driving is another area of concern where common sense should apply but many times does not. My husband was at a busy intersection when a woman made a left turn into a four lanes road with a cellphone in one hand next to her ear, a coffee cup in her other hand, while gripping the steering wheel with her pinkie. Two young children were in the back seats, watching.

I must admit I enjoy my new ability to send text messages.

I have my teenage grandchildren to thank for bringing my thumbs into the twenty first century.

However, I also appreciate the need for respect and common sense to prevail when using texting at home, in the workplace, on the road and in other community settings.

Thumbs up Grandmas and Grandpas! Let the texting begin.

Digital Detox

In a wooded area in Navarro, California, a former Boy Scout campground has a new purpose for only adult campers. It is called Camp Grounded and their motto is Disconnect to Reconnect. It is a device free area. No one is allowed to bring phones, tablets, watches, or any other devices. The campers are not to talk about work, use their real names or ask for people's ages. It is an attempt to have people, hooked twenty four seven to a variety of technology, step away and relate to each other face to face. Looking at the pictures of the campers on the internet, I was struck by the many smiling, laughing, relaxed faces and fun filled activities they seemed to be thoroughly enjoying with each other. The camp is just one of a growing number of programs being developed to help people take a break from the information overload they are experiencing and participate in some temporary form of digital detox.

About five years ago, I started the practice of keeping my computer turned off for a day, once a week, on Sunday. I had begun to get a bit obsessive about checking my email numerous times and wandering around the internet. I had no official name for this practice, just the need to take a break from even my limited involvement with technology. To this day, I have never regretted that decision, and have added the iPad I won about two years ago to that list.

According to a previous report on CNN, Americans spend at least eight hours a day staring at a screen and more than a third of smart phone users get online before they get out of bed. Three years ago, an organization named Reboot, called for a National Day of Unplugging. The purpose was to encourage people not to go online for twenty four hours. The question posed was: Could you power down for just one day? I wonder if some people, who are not in a position to do it for a whole day, could do it for just one hour a week or even once every month.

More people in the workforce are beginning to make concrete plans for their vacation time. They put in place a detailed plan, well in advance, to disconnect from most of the workplace stream of communication. They delegate, give plenty of notice when they will be off line and when they will be back. Dealing with the increasing stress of information overload can seriously affect your overall health in a variety of ways, at any age. It is important to learn how to manage the level of your activity and recognize the need for periodic digital detox breaks.

Sleep Texting

Several years ago, my grandchildren encouraged me to learn how to text. Now, texting has become a key means of communication between me and my sons and grandchildren. With two sons, and their families, living far away, it allows me to get updates, while they are happening, about their sporting events, and other activities. It's the closest thing to actually being at the event itself. Texting is also an easy way to touch base on logistical matters, without requiring a phone call. I appreciate the positive power of it and use it regularly.

However, just about every new technology comes with blessings and curses. This is also true with texting. The latest curse with texting is a bizarre but growing trend I learned about recently called sleep texting.

There is increasing concern, among members of the medical profession, about the health risks associated with sleep texting. One article on WebMD referred to sleep texting as a decidedly twenty first century sleep issue. Because teens and young adults frequently sleep with their phones near or in their beds, they are more likely to be awakened by the sound of the beep.

Half asleep they respond to the caller but have no clear memory of it in the morning.

In a study by Michael J. Breus at the Kaiser Family Foundation: More than half the teenagers who text and use the internet at bedtime are at risk for developing mood, memory and thinking problems during the day. Sleep deprivation over time can lead to several serious health issues including high blood pressure, obesity, depression, behavioral problems and drug abuse. Since the advent of texting, more health professionals are seeing an increasing rise in sleep problems in general, but particularly among the young. A number of health professionals suggest cellphones, computers and other electronic devices be kept out of the bedroom as a way of preventing technology from interfering with teenagers' sleep.

Unlike my grandchildren, I came into the rapidly developing world of technology as an adult. I remember, with a chuckle, when I first was introduced to email in my workplace. I would send the email and then call the person to check to make sure they had received it. There would be the sound of laughter at the other end of the phone!

Tonight, when I go to sleep, my cellphone will be turned off and tucked safely in a drawer. And I will sleep more soundly, in a night world, protected from constant interruptions.

Musings about Twitter

I'll admit I'm new to this whole world of twittering, tweets and hashtags, even though it has been around since 2006. It's only recently I have developed a curiosity to become more informed about it.

I grew up using Webster's Dictionary as my faithful guide and resource for learning the meaning of words. So, just for fun, I checked out Webster to see what it had to say about the word twitter. I chuckled when I read it meant to utter successive chirping sounds or to talk in a chattering fashion or to tremble with agitation. A number of tweets I have read so far seem, in a crazy way, to fit those descriptions! The word, hashtag was not to be found in Webster's Dictionary, which didn't really surprise me.

I feel like I am part of two very different worlds. There was the period of my childhood, before television, and the rapid advances of technology. Now today, technology is upgrading and developing constantly and google.com provides the answers that Webster's Dictionary lacks, and so much more.

So, of course, I turned to google.com in my continuing search to find out more about both the wonderful and wacky world of Twitter Inc. Many of you already are very knowledgeable and use Twitter Inc. However, for those of you like me, here are a few facts I found in my trip through google land. The shortest definition of #Hashtag is a symbol used to mark keywords on topics in a tweet. Twitter Inc. is an online social networking and microblogging service that enables users to send and read short 140 character text messages called tweets. Registered users can send and read tweets, but unregistered users can only read in Wikipedia.

My interest in Twitter Inc. only surfaced very recently when I heard a brief news report about a girl who was born with part of one of her arms missing. Her friends launched a Twitter campaign, #Hand for Torri, in the hopes of raising money for their friend to be fitted with a bionic arm. Their efforts paid off. This story made me realize how much good could be accomplished through Twitter Inc. and that ignited my curiosity about it. In my readings, I saw where #sandiegofire was used to help coordinate an emergency response to a fire. So it can be effectively used as an emergency communication system. It also has been used to organize protests, and to help make TV more interactive. As a result, I have developed a new respect for the variety of positive uses it can have and that helps dispel the silly, vacuous and insulting ways I have seen it used, at times, by some people.

It was not surprising to read in a 2009 report that sixty three percent of Twitter users are under thirty five years of age. In that same report, they listed the five countries that use Twitter the most: China, United States, India, Brazil and Mexico.

As a result of exploring both the pros and cons of Twitter Inc., maybe I'll even send a few tweets one of these days myself.

Plunging Gone Viral

The rapid pace at which new technologies keep developing more gadgets, and expanding services on the ones already in use, amazes me. There are iPods, iPads, iPhones, mobile hot spots, Wi Fi, DSL, fiber optic networks, social networks, to name just a few. I watch in awe at how quickly most people operate these various devices and access a wide variety of information in an instant.

Like all things in life, there are both benefits and drawbacks to these devices. I have read about some people becoming so addicted to their constant use, it sucks the creative energy out of the rest of their day. I watched a couple in a restaurant hardly look or talk to each other. Their attention was totally focused on their own blackberries. Whoever they were communicating with was more important than the person sitting right across from them.

However, recently, I heard the funniest story about the value of the information highway being literally right at your fingertips! Alice, not her actual name, a friend of mine, had a visitor from out of state a few months ago. Her friend had traveled thousands of miles from her home state to Vermont. After she had been in town for about five days, Laurie quietly mentioned she needed to purchase a plunger. Although Alice had a pretty good idea why her friend might need a plunger, she gently questioned her about it. Laurie sheepishly leaned close to Alice's ear and whispered: Well, you don't happen to have one, do you? To which Laurie quickly replied: Of course, we do, what home with children doesn't have one.

After handing the plunger to Alice, her friend disappeared into the bathroom connected to the guest room. She politely declined all offers from Laurie to help her. Fifteen minutes later, Alice returned to the kitchen and handed the plunger back to Laurie with a big smile on her face. She then explained: I went into the bathroom with your plunger and my iPhone. I was too embarrassed to have you help me or to admit I had never used a plunger in my life. I had never even seen it used but I knew they were used to dislodge obstructions in toilets. So, I got on my iPhone and clicked on You Tube. To my amazement, I found twelve different sites with specific instructions describing how to use a plunger. One site even explained the importance of having plenty of water to submerge the plunger in and it all worked to my utter relief.

Plunging gone viral indeed!

Flying the Friendly Skies

I happily boarded the plane and took my window seat. Placing my backpack under the seat in front of me, I sat back and watched as passengers wrestled their luggage into the overhead bins. What some travelers consider as luggage to carry on these days amazes me. It requires a lot of pushing, pulling and literally stuffing with all your might to fit it in the overhead bin so the top will click closed. Meanwhile, passengers wait in frustration as each person goes through this dance.

On this flight, one young woman had a suitcase with stickers all over it. Hanging from a rope tied to the handle of her bag was a large roll of brightly colored duct tape. With all her effort to fit it in an already nearly full bin, the duct tape became the final battleground. I thought the people in line behind her were about to mutiny when, with a final shove, the duct tape disappeared into the bin. I almost felt like clapping.

Every person I know who has ever flown, has at least one hilarious, frustrating or frightening story to tell about their experience. It is not surprising when you consider how busy the airways are these days and the number of people who are flying.

One of my sons had me laughing and, at the same time breathing a sigh of relief, as he retold an experience he had, several years ago, on a flight to Bend, Oregon from Washington. The second leg of his trip from Portland to Bend required he hop a puddle jumper to Bend with what he termed the boy pilot at the controls. The thought of needing air goggles amusingly crossed his mind as mental pictures of Snoopy and the Red Baron emerged. It was snowing and the wind was picking up as they took off in the dark. Once in the air, the pilot announced they would be landing in a small airport with no control tower. Eventually, when they prepared to land, the pilot strongly urged the few passengers on board to hold on tightly because the landing was to be very bumpy. My son watched as the wings of the plane heaved back and forth. He seriously wondered if a wing would hit the ground before the wheels. However, the young pilot managed to make a very bumpy but safe landing. As my son stepped from the plane in a raging snowstorm, he knelt and kissed the ground!

What does concern me when flying these days is, in too many cases, a lack of civility and simple kindness. One recent flight I was on had been delayed in leaving so we were late in arriving at our destination. As we prepared to land, one of the stewardesses made a request. On our full plane there were fourteen passengers with tight connecting flights. She asked that those fourteen people be allowed to deplane first. When we landed just about everyone on board stood up. The stewardess asked again for the fourteen to be allowed to leave the plane first and the others remain in their seats. Not one other person standing had the consideration to sit down. Such a small but helpful request and yet it fell on deaf ears. As one who has experienced tight connections, I felt for those fourteen and wondered afterward how they all made out.

Everyone who flies needs to always bring with them a fully developed sense of humor, more than adequate doses of patience and adaptability and a good supply of simple kindness. Then we can rest assured the friendly skies will remain friendly.

The Value of Observation

I continue to be amazed at the numerous technological advances that have been developed in my lifetime so far. It has brought many conveniences to our everyday lives. Various devices bring instant information and faster forms of communication. The cellphone alone has become so popular, people of all ages now own one. Humorously, I sometimes view it as an extension of a person's arm, especially some teenagers and young adults. You rarely see them without a cellphone held firmly in one hand.

My one growing concern is how cellphone usage has impacted face to face communication, particularly among the young. In one Pew Research article it stated 73% of teenagers own smart phones now and most have come to prefer texting rather than face to face conversations. I totally understand the instant convenience of texting and use it myself. However, the use of it to the growing exclusion of face to face encounters denies young people particularly, the opportunities to learn so much from direct contact with another. A text does not display the full range of emotions and mannerisms you can observe when talking directly with someone. Imogees, those little symbols on a smartphone used by many to display an emotion, are no replacement for the full range of facial expressions.

Young people have become so accustomed to texting, a January 2016 New York Post headline stated: Many New York City students are so tech-oriented they can't even sign their own names. When one of my oldest granddaughters was in seventh grade, living in another state, some years ago, she told me she could not read my hand written letters. She explained that she had never learned to use the cursive form of writing. I was surprised and concerned. Yet she could text at the speed of light.

In a book, titled, Disconnected, by Thomas Kersting, he states his concerns this way: If young folks spend most of their time communicating through text messaging rather than face to face, the brain will weed out the neural pathways that are necessary for becoming a good face to face communicator. There have been articles written about the growing difficulties some young people face when they show up for a job interview and struggle with the face to face reality as they try to interact with a potential employer.

As we continue to advance in our technological capabilities, my hope is that we will not find ourselves, as the saying goes, throwing out the baby with the bath water. The value of face to face communication should never be underestimated in its intrinsic value, regardless of how technologically advanced we continue to become. The importance of regular face to face interactions with people in partnership with responsible use of technology should be our goal as we move forward.

Airline Purgatory

According to Webster's dictionary, purgatory is a place or state of temporary suffering or misery. As I sat in an airport recently, I overheard a humorous conversation between two strangers. Like my husband and I, they were waiting, in a very crowded airport terminal, for a flight that was repeatedly announced as delayed. One man, with a mischievous smile spreading across his unshaven face, stated: Do you think there is an Airline Purgatory and that's where we are now? Cause I've not been that bad to go to hell so this must be purgatory. After five hours of delays, at 9 p.m. that evening, our flight was canceled. I tended to agree with him!

In my experience flying to various family events, flight delays and sudden cancellations are becoming increasingly commonplace. Some Airlines seem to have more problems in this area than others. In addition, there is also the issue of overbooking. During this stay in Airline Purgatory, I heard repeated calls for volunteers to give up their reservation. Some requests came with multiple perks to sweeten the pot. The worst of all, from my perspective, was a request for TEN people, on the same flight, to be willing to change their reservations to another time or even day!

During this same period of travel, I had what I like to refer to as the Granny Pat Down. At age seventy three, sporting gray hair and being the proud grandmother of eight, this Granny was taken aside and told I needed to be patted down. To provide some privacy, I was directed to a storage hallway by two female security personnel. I must say, the process was fully explained to me but humiliating just the same. In fact, during part of it, I just closed my eyes and tried to mentally leave the room. Two weeks later, in another airport, I was told to stand spread eagle, hands above my head and have a full body scan TWICE! According to the overbearing security guard, I had moved during the first one. I've warned all my children to be careful around me as I am now apparently radioactive and a potential terrorist threat!

We were able to rebook our canceled flight to a 6:30 a.m. flight the next morning. Many people slept in the airport that night. We were fortunate enough to have a son living about an hour away, who came and picked us up. After a night's sleep, in a real bed, we arose at 4 a.m. and prepared to head to the airport. Once in the terminal, we learned our flight had a crew to fly it but no plane! You guessed it, delayed yet again!

As I sat waiting for a plane to be found, I heard a hilarious version, from other passengers, of their night spent in the airport. Several of them finally fell asleep, in various awkward positions, only to be suddenly awakened by the sound of a vacuum cleaner moving around them! A family of four, from Houston, Texas, slept in the airport through no fault of their own. The parents had previously made reservations, arrived at the airport and checked in, gone through security with boarding passes in hand with no apparent problems. When they arrived at the terminal podium to board the plane, they were told their boarding passes were invalid. They were stranded till a helpful gate attendant took the time to correct the error the next day!

I must confess, I am not in any hurry to revisit Airline Purgatory anytime soon. However, during my stay there, my faith in humanity was strengthened by a few conscientious airline employees and the support and sense of humor, under duress, of my fellow passengers.

Unsung Heroes and Heroines

Standing Up for Milo

Milo is a sweet faced little boy, with bright blue eyes and a smile that would melt most hearts. He lives in another state with his parents and often eats at a local Italian restaurant.

One day, while Milo and his family were eating, another family, with school age children, came in and sat at the next table. Shortly after they sat down, the father started talking in a loud voice, easily heard by everyone nearby. The waiter, Michael Garcia, returned to check out what the issue was for this man. The customer stated, Special needs people should be served someplace else. This was the mildest of the remarks he made to Michael at that time. You see little Milo has Downs Syndrome.

Michael listened quietly to the man's comments, and while he was listening, he made a courageous decision. He did not know if he could lose his job over his action, but he refused to serve them and told him why. He then reported to his boss what he had done, and rather than a reprimand, the boss fully supported his action. I believe the father decided to take his family to another restaurant, rather than realize what a negative and prejudiced example he was setting for his own children. After so much progress has been made in understanding the needs of people with disabilities, this incident was a painful reminder there are still insensitive people out there who just don't get it.

Somehow, this story became viral and I first heard about it in a news clip one morning, when the waiter, Michael Garcia, was being interviewed. The school, which Milo attends, invited Michael to visit. I think Milo's parents had told the teacher what he had done and the class wanted to thank him. When the story went viral, Michael began to get gifts of money for his courageous act. He gave the money to the school, which has now set up a scholarship fund for the children. At the time of the news report, Michael had received $1,145.00.

This story prompted me to reflect on the whole issue of prejudice and the amazing effects one modest act of courage can have, not just in the moment, but across a community, and even beyond. What I call the ripple effect of one simple act of respect and kindness.

It is a fleeting moment in time that honors the small courageous acts that make the world a better place.

Making a Difference

Although kindness is rarely a job,
it is always an option.
Steve Hartman

What really left the most lasting impression on me these days is not all the negative headlines that bombard us daily. It is short vignettes, discussed briefly in the media, about people who make a choice to reach out and touch another person's life in a positive and sometimes, heroic way. Those stories don't grab headlines but they definitely lift your spirits. It serves as an effective reminder there are so many wonderful people out there going about their daily rounds who are making a difference in a quietly significant way.

There is the touching and memorable story of the repo man. The job involves removing belongings when people fail to make their scheduled payments over a certain time. One day the repo man came to remove a couple's car. He found an elderly couple living alone. They had fallen on hard times due to some health problems. Ultimately, he did his job and removed the car. However, that is only a small part of the story. The repo man went way beyond his normal job description. His heart was moved by the sad plight of this aging couple. He inquired what payments were left on the car and paid them. Then he took the car to get some much needed repairs and paid for that as well. Eventually, he returned the car to the very grateful couple.

I saw another work related story also discussed on a TV program. An eighteen year old boy walked to and from work at a factory every day. Some of his fellow employees noticed this and also that he was a reliable and hard worker and always on time. As they began to interact with him, they discovered he lived quite a distance from the factory. His fellow employees also learned the young man lived with his mother, who was now disabled and unable to work. He was doing his best to provide for his mother and himself. Someone at the plant took the initiative to discuss this teenager's situation with the rest of the employees and organize some means of helping him. They successfully raised enough money to purchase a small jeep. When they presented it to him, the young man was overwhelmed and brought to tears. Now he was able not only to drive to work but also to take his mother to her medical appointments.

The final story is truly a wonderful act of heroism. A policeman apprehended a dangerous fugitive and was wrestling him to the ground. Cars passed by and observed the scene but chose to ignore it. One car stopped as the driver could easily see the policeman needed help. She called 911 to report the incident. She got out of the car and went to assist the officer. Both men were on the ground. The fugitive had the upper hand and was reaching for the policeman's gun. The woman jumped on the back of the fugitive and pulled his arm behind his back and twisted it. The 911 response team arrived and took over the scene but credited the woman with saving the officer's life. This woman saw someone who needed help and did not hesitate to give it. It did not matter to her the officer was a white male and she was an African American female. All that mattered to her was another human being needed help and she was moved to give it.

Steve Hartman was right, kindness is always an option, but oh, what a heartfelt and significant difference it can make to another.

Stepping Up to the Plate

$$\mathcal{CSSO}$$

Nathan is only a thirteen year old boy but already he has saved a life.

It all happened when Nathan was in the locker room getting ready for baseball practice. The coach was seated not far from him. They were alone in the locker room as the other members of the team had finished dressing and ran out on the field to warm up. The coach was talking and laughing with Nathan. Suddenly, without warning, he fell on the floor, face down. Because the coach had a reputation as a prankster, Nathan thought this was some kind of joke. Nathan called to him a couple of times, but he did not respond. He went to his side to check. The coach was not breathing so Nathan quickly called 911, using the coach's iPhone. He turned the coach over and began CPR. By the time the first responders arrived, the coach was breathing again but still unconscious. They quickly transported him to the hospital where he was diagnosed as having had a major, life threatening heart attack. This was a shock to everyone as the coach was an active adult in great shape.

After the coach recuperated, he credited Nathan with saving

his life. The story made the national news. I watched as both the coach and Nathan were interviewed. The members of that baseball team had been given CPR training at the encouragement of the coach. Nathan had been trained what to do and did not hesitate to do it. This made all the difference.

I am continually impressed and uplifted by the stories of the heroes and heroines among us. Whenever I am watching TV or listening to the radio, I pay special attention to the side stories. They are the brief moments when the spotlight is taken away from all the negative news and turned on stories like Nathan's. I view them as a brief but important reminder of the goodness and courage of others, regardless of age.

The story of Nathan also renewed my belief that giving children guidelines in how to deal with certain emergencies is so important. Age appropriate talks or specific training, as was done with that baseball team, can be very helpful. In my work as a community nurse, I dealt with parents with special physical needs. Many of those parents trained their very young children to use the phone and call 911. A young preschooler called 911 when she could not wake up her diabetic mother. Again, in this case, that call made all the difference. Very young children can be given simple instructions while older ones are ready for more detailed instructions, such as CPR.

Nathan did not hesitate to step up to the plate when he was needed the most. When he was asked by the TV interviewer: Were you afraid the coach was going to die? Were you scared? Nathan answered simply: I just focused completely on what I had to do and kept doing it.

On a moment's notice, Nathan brought to this crisis the

knowledge he had previously learned, the courage to act quickly and appropriately and an inner strength to focus on the task.
As a young baseball player, you could say he gave his coach a
very significant home run.

Good Samaritans

Recently, in an attempt to drive into my driveway, I ran into a large pile of snow. It had been left by the street plow at the end of our driveway. It is one of the drawbacks of living on a corner lot. I was unsuccessful so my car remained hung up on the mound of packed snow. I grabbed a shovel and began to dig around the tire, as I waited for my husband to join me. A young man, dressed for running, came around the corner moving at a quick, steady pace. He stopped, came over and offered to help. He took the shovel, began digging and remained digging, even after my husband had arrived and joined him. He didn't have to stop to help in that moment, but he chose to do so. I was very touched by his spontaneous act of kindness.

Shortly after my own experience of being assisted by a passing Good Samaritan, my ears perked up when I heard of two other incidents reported on a TV news program. The only reason these stories made the news was someone was quietly observing them in the background. In a grocery store, in another state, an older man unloaded his groceries on the conveyer belt. The checker began to ring them up on the register. When she told the customer what the total was, he began to remove some of the groceries. He said he lacked the forty dollars to pay the entire bill. The young checker grabbed her wallet and took out two twenty dollar bills. She told the man she would make up the difference and he could take all his groceries. He thanked her profusely and gave her the money he had. The groceries were bagged and he left the store. However, the story does not end there because there was another Good Samaritan standing behind the man. He saw what the checker had done and was so impressed by her generosity of spirit, he reached into his own pocket and gave the checker forty dollars to make up for the forty she had just given away. One kindness had quickly prompted another.

The other story I heard about in the news came a week later. It also took place in another state. A local store owner called the police about a shoplifting incident at his store. A police-man was dispatched to check it out. He found a very frightened woman had stolen three eggs. When he questioned her, she told him, she had two very young children and she and the children had not eaten in two days. The policeman paid for a dozen eggs and drove the woman home. He found a sparsely furnished home and two hungry children. He got the word out that this family was in dire need of some food. The response was over-whelming. Again, a wonderful example of the ripple effect one caring Samaritan can have on others.

There is always one moment, and even more, when each of us is in the position to act as someone's Good Samaritan. It is always a free choice but what a lovely gift to be able to share with a fellow traveler on life's journey.

A Christmas Presence

Whenever you watch a person being interviewed on television who has recently performed what is considered a heroic act, they quickly respond, I'm no hero. I was just doing what needed to be done. Often, they step up to help a perfect stranger or strangers, sometimes at personal risk to themselves. I believe every person is capable of small but meaningful acts of heroism every day. It is a matter of being aware of the environment around you in your family, at work, with friends and in the communities where you live. Not every person is given the crisis moment to perform dramatic acts of heroism. However, each person has numerous opportunities each day to reach out in some small way and have a positive impact on another person, even a stranger.

The Christmas season is the perfect time to bring that sense of caring presence to the people you love and the perfect strangers you meet along your travels. So much focus these days is on the presents, the tangible gifts, why not equal attention to small heroic acts of kindness too? It can be as small as letting a car get in your lane or a person go ahead of you in the checkout line in the grocery store. A compliment to a tired checker can bring a smile that just lifts their spirits. There are so many ways to bring your presence to a situation and make a difference. I always consider these brief moments of reaching out to another like throwing pebbles in a pond. That one small act of caring has a ripple effect reaching out beyond in ways you will never know. The receiver may be prompted by your act of kindness to pay it forward in some way in their own life, the ripple effect.

About two years ago, I came across a Christmas card verse that has stayed with me ever since I read it. It describes Christmas in such a beautiful way. It goes like this: Every time a hand reaches out to help someone, that is Christmas. Every time someone puts conflict aside and strives for understanding that is Christmas. Every time people forget their differences and realize their love for each other that is Christmas.

Families

The Hug

One sign of the times is the use of surveillance cameras in most stores. The stores which have many aisles and lots of merchandise use the cameras most often. It is one way store managers find helpful in trying to keep theft to a minimum or help in identifying the thief. However, sometimes what is captured on the tape is a poignant moment.

Recently, while watching a television news program that frequently airs human interest stories, a video clip from a grocery store camera came across the screen. The people in the clip had given permission for it to be aired and the man in the tape was interviewed for the piece.

An elderly man was standing motionless in the aisle, eyes cast down, as he stared vacantly at the cans on the shelf. He seemed frozen in that position as a young mother came up the aisle pushing a grocery cart. In the cart sat a bright eyed little girl about three years old. As they came upon the man, the little girl stood up and reached out her small arms, and said something to the man. He came closer and she wrapped her arms around his neck.

56

Today is my birthday, can I give you a hug is what the child called out to the man. The man moved forward and let the small child give him a warm embracing hug. That moment had a profound and lasting effect on both the man and the child.

The elderly man was a veteran who had recently lost his wife after many long years of a loving marriage. He quickly lost interest in doing anything and slipped into a depression. The depression was brought on by his grief over the death of his wife. His children and grandchildren were all grown and lived at a distance, with busy lives of their own. He went about the usual tasks with lackluster interest. That day in the grocery store, he was trying to decide what groceries he needed although even his appetite for food had diminished.

When the little girl asked to hug him, he was surprised but willing. Once she placed her warm little arms around his neck, something in his frozen heart melted. The little girl also asked if she could see him again. The mother spoke with the man about setting up a time to visit him at his home the following week. Thus began an endearing friendship between this young child and once grief stricken man. The little girl often brings a book and they sit and read it together.

The enormous power of a simple hug is truly amazing. I have lived long enough to have been the happy recipient of many welcome hugs and in my professional life have respectfully given many a hug. Like that little girl, wise beyond her years, I always ask the person first if I do not know them well. Some people are not always ready for such a close, intimate gesture, no matter how well intentioned.

I think the true heroine of this story is the little girl's mother.

There was a busy, young mother shopping for groceries. She could have ignored the sad, lonely man and her daughter's desire to give him a hug. However, she took the time to stop and that made all the difference. When her daughter followed up the hug with a request to be able to see the man again, she did not hesitate to arrange for a follow up visit with him at his home. As a result of her actions, a very special ongoing friendship was allowed to blossom between this once grief stricken widower and a bright eyed, sensitive young child.

Makes you wonder what might I have done if I were that busy parent walking down the aisle of the grocery store that day?

Bench Buddies

A new school year is in full swing these crisp autumn days. I watch and wave as the yellow bus rolls up our street. The youngest children can hardly see over the bottom of the windows. The scene floods my mind with memories, as I bend down to pick up the morning paper. I recall in vivid detail, the years our three sons rode those big, yellow school buses.

As a young family, we moved to different states several times. Each of our sons had the experience of being the new kid in the different schools they attended. I could relate to the feelings they experienced each time. I had changed schools as a child in both grammar and high school when my family moved to new locations. It's a tough experience to walk into a new school, not knowing anyone. The younger you are the more overwhelming it can feel. My sons now joke about sitting in the lunch room, at a table all by yourself, those first few days, while groups of students are chattering all around you.

Recently, I picked up a magazine that runs a column titled: Pass It On, People Helping People and one topic caught my attention. As I read the article, I kept thinking what a wonderful idea for young children in grammar school. I wondered how it might have been for our sons in those first awkward days at school. The focus of the short article was on the practice, in a school in Germany, of having a Bench Buddy. It was a special bench located on the school playground. The bench was designated for children who felt lonely. They were invited to sit on the bench. This would signal to the other children that the new student wanted an invitation to play.

A family in Pennsylvania had been searching the web for schools in Germany for their young son, Christian. There was the possibility Christian's father might be transferred there for work. While they were looking at one school's website, Christian noticed the bench designated as a buddy bench. He mentioned it to both his mother and his teacher. He thought it was such a good idea because then no child need ever be left out of recess.

The Buck family did not move to Germany. However, they had not forgotten the idea of a bench buddy. The family bought a bench and painted it. With the school's permission, they placed it in the playground where Christian was to attend second grade. The reason for the bench was explained to the students and they adopted the idea fairly quickly. Apparently, the story of the bench buddy started to spread and presently, schools across the country have their own Bench Buddies.

A Chance Encounter

The winter temperature outside was in the teens and it had begun to snow. The young mother hurried with her two children toward the grocery store. She was off from work for a few days and trying to get all the cookie and bread baking done. Like so many other young mothers, Lisa, not her real name, was living the reality of so much to do and so little time. As she neared the entrance to the store, a scruffy, older man with no mittens or socks on his feet and a worn cap on his head put out his hand. He asked if she could spare any change. She kept moving but told him she would see him on the way out.

Mommy, the man looks so cold and hungry, why didn't you give him some money, asked her seven years old child? Lisa explained money was not a wise thing to give the man. Instead, they would pick out some food and hand it to him when their shopping was done. As they left the store, they stopped and handed the man a couple of bagels, a cooked chicken and a can of ginger ale all in a bag.

All the way home in the car the two girls worried about the man out in the cold with no socks or mittens. They kept asking their mother about him. The next day, they went back to the grocery store, picked up some oranges and apples and handed them to the homeless man. In addition to the food, they brought a pair of socks, mittens and an old Army blanket for him. This time the man told them his name was Jerry, not his real name.

Lisa and her daughters have not seen the man again, but it has sparked many dinner conversations. I heard from the parents, the children continue to be curious and concerned. It has prompted discussions about homelessness, how to help and how to be safe when strangers approach you. On cold nights, the children will wonder how the man is doing and refer to him by the name he gave them. Their encounters with Jerry caused them to see him as a fellow human being. He was no longer a faceless homeless man on a street corner.

I have found myself playing this story over and over in my head. This mother's actions and the profound example Lisa has planted in the minds and hearts of her children impressed me very much. So many valuable discussions have sprung from this chance encounter. I also replay the compassion that so instinctively came from the mouths of children so young. They saw the neediness of this human being. These young girls wanted to help. Their mother took the time, in her busy schedule, to guide them wisely through it. What would YOU do?

Perspective

The scoreboard read 3-0. The last period in a youth league hockey game for boys, ages 12 and 13, began with the red team ahead. When the blue team was scored on again, I could not believe what happened. The father of the blue team goalie, face beat red, eyes ablaze in anger, ran from his seat in the stands to the fencing behind his son. He scaled the fencing to its arch above where his son was in position to play. Immediately, he started yelling all sorts of criticisms. He appointed himself coach and screamed instructions at his son. Eventually, he was removed from the arena, but the damage was done. His son was not the only one embarrassed. All of us who watched were held, for a moment, in suspended disbelief.

Now years later, all three of our sons are married with children of their own and here we were again back attending a variety of youth sporting events; this time as loving grandparents.

A little league baseball game had just ended. The ten years old players began to gather around a snack table provided by the parents. I watched as one mother took her child's arm and quickly guided him to their family van. He was given no time for snacks or to bask, with his teammates, in the glory of winning a tough, close game. The door to the van was open so I was able to observe the son stripped of his base-ball uniform. A soccer outfit was put on in its place. Soon after, the van doors closed. The car made a hasty retreat from the parking area. I found out later, from my son, this was a frequently repeated scene for the boy. Every weekend was spent playing multiple games, in a variety of sports. His mother's own dream for her son was that he would become a star soccer player. She had her sights set on a college athletic scholarship.

As I reflected on these two scenes and all the many wonderful experiences children can have when involved in youth sports, I discovered one surprising reality. Winning is everything! However, all of us who are parents or grandparents of children involved in youth sports, need to understand what winning is all about.

Winning is not only what is reflected on a scoreboard. It also involves the life lessons youth sports offers each child to take on the rest of their journey across time. It teaches the benefits of working together as a team. It can be an early and effec-tive lesson in working to reach a common goal. One of my sons, who coaches youngsters, said he appreciates the value of a positive approach; combining a realistic assessment of a player with the expectation he will do his best.

With mature parental guidance and support, youth sports can guide a child in the value of good sportsmanship, responsibil-ity and the personal effort required to improve. Children can learn to have fun along the way and relish the preciousness of the moment. As parents, we must realize we are the first and most powerful role models in our children's lives. Our behavior speaks volumes. They are always watching.

I still wonder what happened to that young goalie.

Choices

I believe life is a series of choices. While our options may be challenging, we still have choices.

In my readings over the years, I was intrigued by true stories about people who overcame difficult, sometimes dangerous circumstances, and never lost their fundamental belief in the beauty of life.

In the book, The Meaning of Life, by Viktor Frankl, the author relates how a prisoner, on a work detail, in a German prison camp, stops to enjoy a sunset. He could have been beaten or worse. He chose to take the risk to reaffirm his basic human dignity.

An unforgettable quote from Frankl's book states: Everything can be taken from a man but one thing, the last of the human freedoms, to choose one's attitude in any given set of circumstances, to choose one's own way.

That quote resonated with me as the result of a recent encounter during a baseball game. The Detroit Tigers were playing the

Cleveland Indians. The Tiger's pitcher, Armando Galarraga, was poised to make baseball history by pitching a perfect game. There were two outs in the ninth inning. The batter hit to the infield. The ball was fielded and thrown to the baseman. The first base umpire positioned himself with the Indians first baseman between him and the runner. The umpire called the batter safe while a clear view indicated, without a doubt, the runner was out. Calmly, Galarraga, though puzzled, went back to the mound with a smile on his face, and finished the game. The umpire headed off the field to watch the replay. When he realized his mistake, he immediately apologized to the pitcher at the end of the game. Jim Joyce, the umpire, also met with the press to admit his mistake publicly. When Galarraga spoke to the press he told them: I feel worse for Joyce than for myself. You don't see an umpire after the game come out and say: Hey, let me tell you I'm sorry. He felt badly.

The pitcher was denied his perfect game technically but what a perfect example these two men set for all the fans, especially young people. They each made a choice how they would react to a tough situation and decided to take the honorable way with great grace and dignity. We need more people like that in all walks of life.

Remember when everyone was in great fear over the H1N1 swine flu? I was at a clinic to get an injection. I witnessed the sweetest act of compassion from a tiny four years old boy. He sat across the room from me with his parents, in a large school auditorium. We had all just been given the vaccination and were waiting the required fifteen minutes for any sign of a reaction. A girl, about eight years old, several rows down, was crying hysterically. I watched as the little boy leaned over to his mother and whispered something in her ear. He got up and walked down to the girl and wrapped his little arms around her. Almost immediately, the girl rested her head on his shoulder. Eventually, she stopped crying. They stood like that for several minutes before the boy released her and returned to his seat. He showed such compassion in one so young. That was his choice, with his mother's insightful permission. It was a heartfelt example of choosing to care and a wise mother granting him her permission to act on it.

Although these are three very different scenarios, they all have a common theme. Three adults and one small child, in very different situations, chose to act with courage and compassion. We are never too young or too old to make the right choices.

Handwritten Thank You Notes

The smallest act of kindness
is worth more than
the grandest intention.
- Oscar Wilde

Are handwritten thank you notes a dying art, a thing of the past, now considered old fashioned? A friend asked me this very question recently. It prompted me to investigate this topic beyond my own initial reactions and thoughts. What I discovered proved quite interesting.

It is not only our own country experiencing a decline in hand written thank you notes. A survey in England revealed it is the fastest disappearing practice in that country as well.

Handwritten thank you notes are becoming a rarity. Many people are now choosing to send short texts or brief emails or no response at all. In one article I read the practice is no longer being passed down to the younger generation. In one online survey of parents, only thirty percent encourage their children to write thank you notes. Another survey, of a thousand adults, found sixty seven percent thought the ability to hand write a thank you note had died out. However, another online poll indicated fifty six percent of those surveyed preferred to receive handwritten thank you notes. So, the desire to receive such a note is still very much alive while the practice continues to decline.

The reality is thank you notes take a lot less time to write than it takes a person to thoughtfully, shop for or make and wrap the gift they have given you. In some cases, it means also wrapping it again to mail and making the trip to the post office to send it to you. The person sending you the gift has spent time, money and thought on that gift. Do you not have a few minutes to write them a note to let them know how much you appreciate them and their gift?

Phone calls, emails, text messages get the job done and are better than no response at all. However, a handwritten thank you note says so much more. It lets family and friends know you went out of your way to sit down and write to them personally. It gives the recipient something they can hold on to and reread. The personal touch of a handwritten note can't be duplicated. It creates a lasting impression as a very personal heartfelt expression of gratitude. It is an excellent way to help children learn the importance of showing appreciation.

The practice of writing thank you notes is not irrelevant or old fashioned. It is simply a thoughtful act of kindness, gratitude and caring.

The Gift That Keeps on Giving

R ecently, I came across one of the first photo albums I had put together as a young child. It was worn with age. Surprisingly, the black and white pictures had not discolored with time and numerous moves. Memories came flooding back to me of a little girl, about eight years old, with long dark black braids. She held a Kodak Brownie Box Camera in her hand. I was so proud of that camera. I took pictures of family, friends, pets and dolls at every opportunity! As I leafed through the pages of the album, many of the chapters of my early child-hood were revisited once again. That's the unique beauty of photos. They allow you to visually open the door to your past for another peek.

When our three sons were grown and no longer living at home, I remember spreading three large plastic bags of photos across a ping pong table. A stack of photo albums sat waiting at the other end. I sat by the table and began a long and poignant trip down memory lane. Just as in real life, it involved much laugh-ter and some tears. A busy family life and multiple geographic moves had delayed this project for years. It seemed like a good transitional activity to take on at that juncture of my life. I was still working outside the home. The weekends found me leaning over the pictures for several hours each Saturday morning. You live your life only once, but pictures make it possible to relive it, in a different form, all over again. It's truly a journey of the heart. It is a powerful process in transitioning from one chapter of your life to the next.

We have come such a long way in photography since my youthful days, snapping pictures with my little camera. Digital and cellphones makes it possible to take the picture and view it in an instant. No more waiting for film to be developed. A picture can be sent to another person just seconds after it is taken miles away. There is one young family I know who sends frequent photos to grandparents by cellphone and email. However, they never thought of saving any to put in an album for themselves! I have often wondered if many other young couples do a similar thing now.

Family photo albums have an intergenerational link. I am constantly reminded of this when my sons and their families visit us. Out come the albums and groups of adult children and grandchildren pour over them with great delight. I am amused by young children's reaction to the pictures of their own parents as babies, young children and teenagers. I broke out in laughter when one of my grandchildren, once commented, Gram, your hair is totally black in this picture!

Shell Collecting

One should lie empty, open,
Choiceless, as a beach,
waiting for a gift from the sea.
-Anne Morrow Lindbergh

Collecting seashells has been a favorite pastime of mine since I was a child. The variety of shells available on a beach fascinates me. As a city kid from Brooklyn, I had the good fortune to spend summers by the ocean. I often got up just before sunrise, quickly dressed, and headed to the beach. My doll, Shelly, was under one arm, and a net bag hanging from my hand.

In those days of my youth, during the summer months, I was given much more freedom to roam by myself. My parents had one rule; never go swimming without an adult family member present. I delighted in walking the beach as the sun rose and cast its light on the treasures from the sea. Though I loved being around people, I also relished the peaceful solitude of walking on a beach alone. Even now, in adulthood, whenever I am near a beach, I still take those early walks at sunrise.

Throughout my life, shells have held much symbolism for me. Shells which arrive on the beach in perfect shape, after all their travels through the various ocean tides and storms represent durability and strength under pressure. Some creatures that inhabit those shells will outgrow them and leave. They are seeking a larger, more appropriate size shell to house them. How similar to how most of us grow up, under the shelter and protection of our families. Then we become adults ready to head out the door.

As a young, married mother with three small children, I was very influenced by Anne Morrow Lindbergh's book, Gift from the Sea. The author, a young mother herself, wrote about specific shells and the symbols they represent for the numerous states and stages of life. That book became a travel guide for me through the various chapters of my own motherhood. Passages were underlined throughout and often read and reread for their enduring wisdom.

Much later, in my life, I was given another book about seashells that has become another guide for dealing with the realities of aging. It was a timely birthday gift from a friend. It is titled: My Beautiful Broken Shell by Carol Hamblet Adams, a writer and shell collector. The beautiful illustrations in the book are by Doris Morgan.

Carol was out walking on a beach and collecting some shells one day. She picked up a broken scallop shell and dropped the less than perfect shell back on the beach. Then she started to realize that she too had some imperfections and reached back down to take the broken shell back. She came to appreciate all that shell had endured as it was tossed and turned in the busy life of the ocean. Even in its less than perfect state, there remained a unique beauty about this shell. This became a metaphor for Carol in her own life, with its own imperfections, challenges and changes over time.

Now, on my desk, there are some perfect shells from my youthful days of shell collecting and several less than perfect shells from more recent beach walks. In the timeless words of Anne Morrow Lindbergh, they are gifts from the sea, strong symbols representing hope, strength, durability, change and enduring beauty, in all its various forms.

A Graduation Speech Perspective

Most graduations occur in the spring and early summer months of May and June. Over the years, I have attended a number of them; some outside in the pouring rain, or the sweltering heat, some on a perfectly beautiful day, or in an enclosed, air conditioned area. At each one, there is a particular person invited to give the graduation speech. Often, these speakers are well known individuals who have made their mark in a particular field. Their audience is the faculty, excited graduates, family members and friends.

This year, I sat in an arena used mainly for concerts. It had a roof but otherwise was open to an unusually chill wind blowing from one side of the complex to the other. With the wind came a snowfall of yellow pollen. There were over seven thousand graduates seated below and many more guests seated in the stands. When the speaker came to the podium, a large and very enthusiastic applause rippled across the arena. The speaker was well known and everyone anticipated a worthwhile speech. By anyone's measure, the speech was totally inadequate and uninspiring. What a missed opportunity! When the speech ended, the applause was polite but lackluster.

Many graduation speeches are quickly forgotten in the excitement of the moment because they were either too long, filled with too many useless platitudes, delivered poorly or just plain uninspiring. The memorable ones often leave you with a theme that grabs you or a one liner that often revisits you long after graduation day has come and gone. In 2005, the writer, David Foster Wallace gave the graduates of Kenyan College a one liner that has stood the test of time. He told the graduates to step outside of themselves, to imagine the values and richness of every life, even when you are standing in line at the supermarket.

I watched a few of the graduation speeches given around the country on TV. Some were excellent, using humor, life stories and an outstanding delivery. However, in a few cases, the speakers used the opportunity, with the captive audience in front of them, to make one sided political commentary.

The most uplifting speech I watched on TV was not a graduation speech. It was given by Mayor Greg Fischer of Louisville, Kentucky shortly after the death of Muhammad Ali. It moved in graduated steps through his life from Ali, the man, to Cassius Marcellus Clay, Jr., the newborn baby, who would be totally unaware of the millions of people he would one day inspire. Mayor Fisher then brought the talk smoothly back to the youth of today and Ali's message of love, peace, compassion and the six core principles Ali lived by. The mayor invited everyone to help today's youth realize their full potential, saying there is no excuse to do anything less. The speech was both a heartfelt tribute to Ali and a call to action for both the young and young in heart.

Every speech, no matter what the occasion, provides a unique opportunity to reach out and inspire people in a significant way. Delivered with sincerity and conviction, an effective speech can convey hope, words of wisdom and so much more. Standing at the podium at a graduation, a speaker is looking out at the future citizens and leaders of the United States. Some graduates may even be listening carefully to what is being said that day. That speech could be imparting a worthwhile message that leaves a deep and lasting impression on those graduates.

What Every Parent Needs to Know

⁓⸎⁓

The same week I purchased my first Smartphone and began the exciting task of learning how to use it, I started to read a ninety one page paperback book, titled, Disconnected. It is written by Thomas Kersting, a prominent psychotherapist. He has years of experience in private practice and as a public school counselor. The sub title on the book cover is How to Reconnect Our Digitally Distracted Kids.

The book is divided into three parts, each filled with compelling information backed up with credible studies. Part One of the book is titled: The Impact of Electronic Devices on Kid's Brains. Studies have shown a link between excessive online use to problems related to depression, anxiety and behavioral issues. In one study, it describes actual changes to the brain. All three parts of the book contain several chapters with specific topics describing: how overuse of online media negatively impacts our children's ability to concentrate, verbal and social skills offline, general self-esteem issues, and in some cases, can lead to a serious addiction.

The second part is titled: Technology's Effect on Social, Emotional and Family Growth. It deals with the video game issue. Mr. Kersting discusses what he titles Gamer Kids: The Great Human Disconnect. Overuse of video games has led to some serious emotional issues for children and their family. This part of the book describes the impact of technology on family life in a variety of ways. There is the growing reality of everyone at a dinner table with their iPhones on reduces direct eye contact and verbal conversation during a shared meal.

Part three of the book concentrates solely on providing parents with numerous ways to help their children benefit from the positive aspects of technology while avoiding the serious pitfalls of overuse. The author titles this section, What Parents Can Do: Tips, Techniques and Solutions.

As I sat reading this book at a doctor's office one day, I had the opportunity to observe a mother and teenage daughter enter the area. The daughter left to go to the rest room while the mother came and sat across from me. The mother immediately pulled out her iPhone. When the daughter returned she looked at her mother for a minute and then pulled out her phone. For the next half hour I was there, this mother and daughter never spoke to each other or had eye contact but stayed totally focused on their phones. It was a reminder of how powerful a role model a parent can be for their children both in negative and positive ways. Parents, in fact all of us, need to take stock of our own online use to make sure we are not slipping into overuse as well. We are role models even when we are not directly parenting children.

I love the benefits of technology but I also appreciate the

importance of staying informed about some of the negative aspects of it as well. Informed parents can serve as a powerful trail guide for their still developing children who are growing up in this fast paced technological world.

The Gift of Time

Recently, two different short video clips came across the TV screen that made me laugh and also had a valuable message. Time spent together is precious and should be treated that way. They were sponsored by an independent nonprofit organization dedicated to helping families travel the world of technology and media in positive ways. One clip showed a baseball team sitting around a table eating, talking and laughing together. At the same table, one teammate was totally removed from the group interaction. He was constantly texting with someone on his cellphone. One of the teammates held up a basket with all his teammate's cellphones in it and invited him, in a friendly teasing way, to join the group. He did and then you see everyone laughing and interacting with each other as the clip ends with the headline: # Device Free Meal.

The second clip really got me laughing as a grandmother with eight grandchildren. All my grandchildren have their own devices and many of them have helped me in the use of mine. In fact, I won an iPad when I bought several tickets to a fundraiser for my oldest grandson's lacrosse team! I still use it now several years later. The video clip depicts grandparents welcoming their children and grandchildren to their home for a meal. As they enter the house, the grandparents have the hallway set up as if you are going through a security check point in an airport. The teenage boy is checked from head to foot and there in one of his socks hides the cellphone! At the very last check point, Grandma has a wand and moves it over a stuffed animal and sure enough there is a cellphone in the belly of the toy doggie. The five year old girl holding the stuffed animal looks grief stricken. You see the logo at the end of the clip: #Device Free Meal.

When you sit down to share a meal with others, it is so much more than just eating some delicious food. Time spent with others you are connected to in some way is also about being present to each person at the table, free of distractions. Everyone participates, both by talking and also listening to the other people at the table. It is a wonderful time to really look at the people around you and observe their facial expressions and mannerisms as they speak. It provides a moment for laughter and lightheartedness. Shared mealtimes are a brief moment, in a busy life, to fully enjoy being together.

Give some thought to having device free meals, with the intention of being more fully attentive to the people sharing the meal with you. You'll be surprised what a gift of time and presence it truly is for everyone.

The Gift of Tears

∞

The assignment in the Art Department woodshop class at the University of Utah was to build something dealing with social interaction. A very innovative student, Nemo Miller, came up with the idea of creating a Cry Closet. It would be for stressed out students to use while studying for final exams. She enlisted the help of her father and uncle in the project. The closet walls were padded with soft fabric, adjustable lighting and a timer. There was also a rug and several stuffed animals. Any stressed out student could only use the closet for ten minutes. It was installed in the library of the university on a temporary basis.

I was not surprised to read that this project was met with mixed reactions by the student body. One student put a picture of the Cry Closet on Twitter and remarked: my school installed a Cry Closet in the library. What is higher education? Her tweet went viral and was shared 174,000 times.

Although I admire the art student's creativity, I still wonder about the overall message of a Cry Closet. Can a person time their sadness? Is holding a stuffed animal a better solution than seeking support from a trusted friend or trained counselor depending on

84

the level of your stress when you are a young adult? Will isolating yourself on a timer help you when you are faced with stressful situations in the workplace or other aspects of your adult life?

It is an interesting topic, worthy of discussion on several levels. As someone who once was a stressed out college student between the ages of eighteen and twenty two, I remember practically living in the library at exam time so I could focus on studying. I also remember going back to college in my forties. So I am not unsympathetic to the stress students feel. It is real but it is also a small slice of what they will need to learn to face in their lifetime.

There is no shame in tears. In fact, they help release the built up tension one feels when under pressure and at other times, they are signs of pure joy and happiness. As a mother of three and grandmother of eight, who spent most of my working life in two service connected fields; nursing and counseling, tears to me are a gift. They open the door to the heart of the matter for so many people and out flows the words locked deep within them. Tears heal in many ways. I have seen it within my family, among friends and also in my interactions with patients and clients who I have worked with in the past.

Much has been written about the increasing social isolation present in our society these days. Some of it is due to the many technical devices that find people spending more time texting or tweeting rather than interacting directly in face to face contact. It continues to make me wonder if encouraging young college adults to sit in a box alone for ten minutes is the best approach to handling the stress of exams.

Guess Who Is Going to Summer Camp!

~~~~~~~~~~~~~~~

One day while randomly surfing the internet, I clicked on a website to check it out. This is the season when the ads for children, teenagers and even some family summer camps begin to surface in magazines and newspapers. However, it was my first introduction to learning about the increasing number of summer camps for adults only.

The website, www.adultsummercamps.com, listed ten pages of camps plus more if you chose to continue your search. I was amazed to read the American Camp Association states half a million adults attend summer camp every year. In 2014, there were about 800 adult camps which was apparently a 10% growth in the number of those camps in the last ten years. I have read about the significantly increased levels of stress people feel in today's fast paced, technological world. I just wondered if the need to get away from it all in an adults only world has increased with this accelerated lifestyle so many families are living today.

The adult camps have a wide range of offerings. There are jazz camps, circus and fantasy themed camps, cattle herding and outdoor recreation camps, sports, music, performing arts, weight loss and spiritual camps to name just a few. I also discovered my own alma mater, Nazareth College in Rochester, New York, has run a jazz camp the last week in July for several years now.

The cost for these camps has a wide range of options. There are short three day stay camps for $150 all the way to a week long camp, with upscale housing, for as much as $2,700. The most obvious way to find the right camp is a google search. It was noted that in any search for adult camps to make sure it is ACA accredited and check what level of fitness or skill level is expected of any potential camper. It sounds like basically the same advice you would follow for any camper, regardless of age.

There is a camp called Camp Grounded which is specifically for adults who feel overwhelmed, and even addicted, to their various gadgets. When you come to the camp, they ask you to either not bring iPhone, iPad, computer, etc. or give them to camp staff to store safely away until you are ready to depart from the camp. The focus of the camp is to have fun and learn to detox from the 24/7 need to check various gadgets. Campers say, after they leave the camp, they return to their regular life with a new sense of being in charge of their technology, not the reverse.

Some adult camps advertise the opportunity for mature campers to get the chance to act like kids again and renew some cherished memories of their youth. Campers enjoy having fun and making new acquaintances beyond their usual circle of friends where they live and work. Campers love the chance to pursue an interest, like playing an instrument with a group, learning how to clown, etc. Quite often, campers report continuing to enjoy these activities at home as hobbies and stress relievers.

Guess who is going to summer camp? It is not only the young but the young at heart as well.

Here's A Radical Thought

A recent conversation with one of my sons rekindled my interest in the rapidly growing use of iPhones. He is presently coaching a girls' ice hockey team. He and his wife hosted a spaghetti supper for the team. It is a way to help the girls spend time off the ice in a social setting, getting to know each other better and having some fun together. Scott took a basket around and asked each girl to put her iPhone in it. He told the girls they could take their phones back when it was time to go home. The parents were told the reason he had done this and he gave them his home number if they needed to be in touch with their daughter. Much more conversation and shared laughter took place among the girls rather that each hooked to their phone, conversing in distracted sound bites.

I also recalled a cartoon I had seen on the internet, titled, A Visit with Grandma and Grandpa. Several adult children and grandchildren sat on a sectional couch in a semicircle. The grandparents sat in the middle of the group. Every single person was focused on their iPhone, texting someone. No one was talking with the people around them. The cartoon was amusing but sad at the same time.

I admire the multiple uses of the iPhone, but I am also increasingly aware of the impact it is having on spontaneous and thoughtful conversations. I read recently there are now 94 million iPhones in use in the United States. Signs have appeared in several waiting rooms, post offices, etc. requesting that iPhones be turned off. I have observed some people in restaurants texting throughout a meal. Why even bother going out with others if your attention is diverted constantly?

So here's my radical thought for the holidays that are coming our way in the weeks ahead. How about when we gather with family and friends to share a meal and time together, we pass around a basket and each person puts their iPhone in it. I realize there are exceptions to this activity. People on call for medical reasons or safety reasons may need their phones kept on and handy. I have had my own days, in the past of being on call during holiday weekends. What a gift it would be to have an essentially iPhone free zone for gatherings of family and friends. Imagine getting and receiving someone's undivided attention during a conversation. Different generations, freed from distractions, able to really listen, share stories, and interact in a more meaningful way. Now that would truly be something to be thankful for and it's totally cost free.

The Elders

The email arrived, addressed in the now familiar way, Dear Elders. It was sent to the group of mature adults who had volunteered one fall for a program at Tuttle Middle School in South Burlington.

In September, my twelve year old granddaughter invited me to consider participating in the intergenerational program scheduled to run monthly throughout the school year. I happily agreed. It would involve meeting with a group of four to six eighth graders for one hour every month. In the letter my granddaughter gave me, the program was described as a year-long initiative of fostering a relationship across generations. The monthly meetings are called reunions and the adult volunteers are referred to as The Elders. Each month The Elders, as well as the middle school participants, are emailed information on that month's topic, readings to be shared with the group and an activity to be completed during the get together. No devices such as iPads, computers or iPhones are to be used during those meetings. The goal is to encourage conversation, direct interaction and eye contact among the members of the group while having some fun as well.

The program, Reaching Out with Reading, Sharing Our Stories, was developed and is implemented by Amy Blauvelt, a librarian and Lori Centerbar, a teacher, both at the middle school. They are present at every meeting to aid and assist members of each group and evaluate how the sessions are going. They are wonderfully supportive and engaging.

The last time I walked into a middle school was for a parent teacher conference for my youngest son. That was years ago and he is now married with two children of his own. So that November day of the first scheduled reunion, I had a few butterflies wondering how this was all going to work out. Then I thought of all the wonderful experiences I have shared with my grandchildren, and still do, and the excitement of the moment came quickly back. I viewed it as an unusual opportunity to meet and get to know some new young people with interesting stories of their own.

Each group has the option to break up into pairs to do the reading, discuss it and report back to the whole group. The other choice our group preferred was to stay together and do the readings and discussion together. Each person takes a turn reading a portion of the topic aloud to the whole group. At various times we stop to discuss what has been read. Both the students and the Elder in the group are encouraged to share their thoughts, reactions and experiences related to the reading.

Programs such as this one provide a very valuable service. It gives those eighth graders a chance to put aside all the technology for a brief period and engage with a person from another generation in activities that are both interesting and fun. For the Elder it is a unique chance to meet and interact with some new young people and hear from them in a friendly and inter-active setting. In my book, that's a definite win.

*Friendship
and
Memories*

Friendship's Garden

Some people come into our lives and quickly go.
Some stay for a while
and leave footprints on our hearts
and we are never, ever the same.
Flavia

In a recent conversation with my fourteen year old grand-daughter, she talked about her plans to attend an overnight camp for a week this summer. She expressed both excitement and some concerns. This would be her first experience staying overnight at a camp for a full week. She was a bit anxious about arriving at this camp not knowing anyone who would be there. As we talked, I explained to her that not knowing anyone could turn out to be a wonderful opportunity. Only last fall, she had been the new kid in school, recently moved to Vermont, feeling some of those same concerns. Yet, in a short time, she met other classmates and developed some wonderful friendships.

In all the many moves I have made over my lifetime, cherishing old friendships and cultivating new ones always felt like tending a beautiful and diverse garden. There are those special people you meet along your journey that remain friends forever, even with the challenges of time and distance. In a garden, they are the hardiest plants, arriving every spring season to visit and delight you. They return year after year because you tended to them in several ways throughout the year. When geographic distance interrupts the easy getting together of good friends, finding other ways to stay connected is very important. What fun it is to have a chance to visit a friend you have not seen face to face in a long time. There isn't a moment of awkwardness, conversation flows and the warmth of the continuing friendship is obvious.

The most beautiful and interesting gardens I have seen in my travels are filled with a variety of plants. Some flowers have many different, vibrant colors and textures. There are the perennials, once planted, return season after season. The annuals need to be chosen and planted yearly. In any healthy garden, you will observe plants and flowers of varying ages and stages. The diversity of friendships is equally important in all areas throughout one's lifetime.

While getting my hair cut recently, my very wise hairdresser had a telling observation about friendships. She described a number of people she has met in her business who retain the same circle of friends. They expressed no interest in making new ones, particularly younger ones. What a missed opportunity was her short but insightful conclusion.

Some experiences bring us into contact with people I will call passing acquaintances. As Flavia describes, some people come into our lives and quickly go. However, the short lived encounter can leave us with a new skill they taught us or a gem of encouragement they said in passing which proved to be very helpful. Sometimes it can just be an interesting conversation or a child teaching us a game on a train or plane as we pass the time seated next to each other. Being open and receptive to these brief connections also leaves us richer in spirit.

Waiting

Recently, I took a seat in the surgical outpatient waiting area of our local hospital. I looked around the room. Each person there was waiting. Some were waiting to have a procedure done. Other people would eventually be called to meet with the doctor to hear the results concerning a loved one or friend. I sensed an unspoken heaviness in the air as I sat there. My husband was undergoing general anesthesia to have a biopsy taken of a growth in his left kidney. The heaviness that hung in the air also had taken up residence in my heart.

With time on my hands and no desire to read or write, I began to reflect on how much waiting is a part of our daily lives in so many small and significant ways. There are the many routine moments of waiting we do daily, waiting in line at the store, the bank, the post office, or for a red light to change to green. Then there are what I call the more significant ones, waiting for a baby to arrive, waiting for a child to return home, waiting in a hospital as I was doing.

The interesting thing about waiting is the emotion each person attaches to it. This ultimately determines how that individual reacts to the need to wait. I have observed all sorts of reactions to just waiting in line at a supermarket. Some people will stand quietly. Others will engage the person behind them to help pass the time. Then there are the ones grumbling under their breath agitated at having to wait at all. Each person brings their own individual brand of coping skills to even the smallest moment of waiting.

The people sitting in the waiting room were from all walks of life and various ages. A young boy sat at small round table with his parents, playing. I could see he had the hospital wrist band on which meant he was the patient due to have a procedure that morning. As the parents played with him to help him deal with the waiting, you could see the lines of concern on their faces. Waiting was a dual challenge for them that day. They had to help their child deal with it at the same time manage their own feelings.

I watched another scene play out between what I assumed was a grandmother and grandson. The grandmother was elderly, bent and sitting in a wheelchair. The grandson, in his twenties, was very slender, high energy, and speaking on an iPhone. He was complaining right in front of the woman that he could not continue to sit and wait with her and he wanted the person on the phone to come and relieve him. The grandmother sat silent, with her head bent. The man made several calls. He told the older woman someone wanted to talk to her. I heard the elderly woman say, Well, I'm very disappointed and gave the phone back to the grandson. The woman turned her head away from him. I saw her wipe several tears from her eyes. Not long after that last call, the woman was taken in for whatever procedure she was scheduled for that day. That young man had a lot to learn about what a privilege it is to give the gift of your time and attention to a loved one.

The act of waiting is a great teacher if we allow ourselves to be its willing, attentive pupils.

Friendship's Legacy

*It is in the shelter of each other
that people live.
Irish Proverb*

I stood at the gravesite of a dear friend as her casket was slowly lowered into the earth. Beset with health challenges since her early twenties, she nevertheless took life by storm. She lived with much spirit, courage, humor and a good dose of feistiness. Those of us who knew and loved her stood in awe of her ability to rise repeatedly above the trials of serious illness. She would resume her travels, work and life with family and friends. However, at the young age of 52, she died, her body just too worn out to fight another day.

Friends come and go in our lives in various ways but our experience with them leaves a profound imprint. Genuine friends are unwitting teachers for each other. In friendship, there are opportunities to deepen our sense of mutual trust and take comfort in the give and take of being truly heard and understood. It challenges us to learn how to deal with conflict and difference of opinion. Do we only hang around with like minded people or do we reach out to people who are different from us in some ways? How much are we willing to give in our friendships? Are we aware of how much we may expect in return?

I have lived long enough to have experienced the death of several very good friends. Each time someone dies and our relationship ends, I find myself struck by how much their spirit continues to live on in me. I draw daily strength from things they have said or done or provided by the example of their lives.

Sometimes, people hesitate to reach out to another in friendship for several reasons. I think that is a lost opportunity. At the end of a year living in Michigan with my husband and children, a woman, in the neighborhood where we had been living, approached me at a farewell party. She expressed regret she had not allowed herself to cultivate a friendship with me. The reason she gave was too many people come and go in that neighborhood. She said she could not deal with the pain of saying goodbye to another friend. How sad, we both lost a whole year's experience with each other. She had been initially so helpful in orienting me to the area but then she totally withdrew.

Real friendship requires a degree of vulnerability. Unfortunately, sometimes the risk of being hurt or suffering loss overpowers the desire to reach out to another. The enduring legacy of genuine friendship is that it endures beyond time and circumstance. We are rich beyond material measure as a result of our friendships.

Focus on What's Important

Several people have spoken to me about how rushed and overwhelmed they feel these days. Even as I go about my daily shopping rounds, I notice few smiles and a number of people rushing about as if they were on permanent speed dial. If the holiday season was meant to give us a meaningful pause, it could develop into another layer of stress for people who already have overloaded lives. I heard one woman say to another how glad she will be when all these holidays are over. How sad.

At the age of twelve, my last memory of my father was of him laughing and joking with me. We were watching a political convention on our twelve inch black and white TV. He was imitating, in humorous ways, some of the cast of characters preening in front of the TV screen. Several hours later, my forty five year old father lay dying from a massive cerebral hemorrhage. I am forever grateful I took the time to sit and enjoy what would be our last and final hours together. That's what I mean about focusing on what's important on any day but also at this busiest of holiday seasons.

I had another kind of poignant reminder of this in a very different set of circumstances. It was not concerning a family member but a complete stranger. I was in the grocery store concentrating on the rest of my day's to do list while unloading my groceries on the conveyor belt. I heard an elderly woman behind me say in a low voice, I have lost the people I came with. I had two choices. I could pay no attention, pay for my groceries and leave. I made the second choice, and turned to check it out. The woman looked frightened and confused. She knew her name but nothing else. A woman behind her also chose to get involved and went to the customer service desk to ask for help. I walked the elderly woman over to the customer service desk. Another woman went ahead of the line there to ask them to make an announcement and mention this woman's name. I waited with the distressed woman to make sure she connected with the people who knew her. Eventually, the driver of the van that had brought her from an adult care facility arrived at the desk. He took her gently by the arm and led her to the van waiting outside the store. Three people chose to take the time to help a complete stranger. That, to me, is the true meaning of this holiday season, focusing on what's important with family, friends, and yes, even complete strangers.

A Season and a Reason

∞

The stores are already gearing up for the holiday season. People will be traveling, in some cases, long distances to spend time with family and friends, celebrating the various holidays. Sometimes those gatherings are totally joyous and filled with laughter and good conversation. However, that is not always the case.

A number of years ago, I read a short essay by a person who preferred to remain anonymous. It was filled with candor and wisdom concerning the challenges of relationships. I clipped it out of the paper and saved it. I refer to this article myself and have, through the years, shared it with others. I think it has a timely message for all of us now as we head into this holiday season:

I wish I could claim that all the people whom I have loved have always loved me back, or that my needs and those of the people closest to me have always dovetailed perfectly. But family and friendship doesn't work that way, and people's needs aren't always the same, so it's only fair to say I have often wished for more, or wished for something no one had to give, and in that I am not alone.

Some people feel angry when they think of moments when they've had to stand alone, and question the value they once put upon friends who weren't there when they needed them. But I think the thing to remember is, you don't get from your friends what you give them, you get what they have to give, and that is the thing you must not forget. People can only give what they have to give.

It is difficult to remember this when you know just what you need and none of your friends have it to give, especially difficult when you have given it to them in the past. But you will save yourself a lot of grief if you keep in mind that you don't have you for a friend, however much you might wish you did. You have that person out there instead.

Perhaps you will take chicken soup to a friend who is sick, and they will forget your birthday just the same. Or maybe you will have them to your parties and they will give none to witch you might be asked. But maybe they will hand you a piece of truth one day, in a sentence tossed off with a sidelong glance, and if it's something you couldn't have found inside yourself, you have been repaid in full.

The holidays offer a golden opportunity for each of us. Wherever we are in the company of others, we can both experience and share a genuine sense of healing and thankfulness and be the positive change, in our small corner of the universe, that we often hunger for in the world at large.

I Don't Know What to Say

Recently, I listened to a very powerful sermon on loss. It dealt with how each of us has experienced loss in our lives and how we have reacted to the losses experienced by others. It also explored the challenge some people feel when dealing with someone's grief and pain. A number of people will avoid visiting a grieving person because they have no idea what to say to them. They fail to appreciate the power of just showing up. A grieving person will often not remember what was said exactly to them. They do remember you were there to sit with them, hold their hand, or give them a warm and caring hug and just be in the moment with them.

I began to recall a moment in time when the presence of someone had meant so much to me. I was a young mother, with one small son, when I lost a baby half way through my pregnancy. After a two day stay in the hospital, I came home feeling a hollow emptiness and deep sadness. A young mother I barely knew came to visit me. She had a container of homemade soup which she quietly placed in the refrigerator. Then she came over and asked if she could give me a hug. She held me in a warm embrace and said: I am so sorry. Those simple gestures meant so much. I never forgot the impact they had on me at the time. My closest friend, also a young mother, never came to visit me. I learned months later, she was overwhelmed by feelings of inadequacy because she felt she didn't know what to say.

As a young student nurse, I remember the Christmas Eve I stayed in the hospital room with the parents of a young son who was dying. They each held one of his hands as he took his last breaths. I stood nearby quietly. After he died, they turned to me and asked if they could pray out loud for him. I reached over and took the hand of the mother and of the father and formed a little circle. They each squeezed my hand tightly and we stood for a few moments in total silence, then they offered their prayer. It's the littlest gestures that can mean so much in a time of such acute loss and sadness. The intent to convey a sincere and heartfelt sense of caring and compassion mean the most to people in the acute stages of grief. There are no precise words one needs to know to say to a person who has suffered a loss. Just being present with them speaks volumes.

We tend to focus on death when the topic of loss comes up but there are many other kinds of loss a person can experience over a lifetime. There is the loss of a job or one's health or home. I still can recall the feelings of fear and horror when I was separated from my parents and sister for twenty four hours in a flood. I was just sixteen years old and had gone to the movies with a bunch of friends. When we tried to drive home later, the roads were flooded and impassable. All communication was lost and there were no cellphones. It was the longest, most terrifying night of my life. The next day, we walked five muddy miles to get back home. Our house was flooded but my family was safe. That was all that mattered to me. I remember running and hugging a woman I initially thought, from a distance, was my mother. I apologized profusely. She just looked at me, with a big smile and said: Honey, that's just what I needed today.

Hidden Treasures

～～

This has been a very long, cold winter. I decided it was the perfect time to go through closets, drawers and storage boxes and make some decisions. Some people call it decluttering. I chose to humorously name it my own personal archaeological dig.

As I opened boxes that had been filled and stored away in our basement, I made some heartwarming discoveries. Of course, this meant, the overall project took longer than initially planned. The hidden treasures in some of those storage boxes were precious. I discovered letters handwritten by our children. What a treat to read again and revisit their youth in my memory. So much of communication today is via email or text. One of my sons recently said to me: Mom, there is something so unique and special about a handwritten letter. I agree.

Any genuine archaeological dig also involves a lot of digging through dirt and debris. Mine was no exception. I had stored away some papers and other artifacts that could be easily disposed of now. They were totally out of date and serving no useful purpose. I set up three large cardboard boxes and labeled them. One was for recycling, another for disposal and the third for articles to be given to family members and others.

I have read that if you have not used an article of clothing or some household item in over two years, it is time to recycle them if they are still useable. Otherwise, it is time to dispose of them. I did a fair amount of both this time around and it is amazing how much lighter it made me feel.

I came across a box with a number of journals I had written in over the years. Those journals took me back on trips and places we had lived I had not thought about in quite a while. I heard again, the voice of the young, working mother laced through some of those journal entries. Lots of humor and hope filled most of the pages. However, there were journeys through loss and sadness as well.

I rediscovered a long misplaced photo of my six foot tall father standing beside me on a beach in Connecticut. I was just five years old at the time. He had taught me to swim. Some adults, on the beach, were worried I would develop polio because I spent so much time in the water. There were many groundless fears regarding polio in those days of my early childhood. My teasing father, with an Irish gleam in his eyes, reassured them not to worry because I was part fish. My father died suddenly when I was just twelve so rediscovering that little black and white photo and the memory attached to it meant a great deal to me.

Living in the present and the uniqueness of each new day is what gives life its real meaning. However, an occasional archaeological dig and brief trip into the past is well worth the time and effort. You come through the journey lighter and you didn't have to give up chocolate! You also have a greater appreciation of all the past experiences that have touched your life and influenced you in so many areas along the way.

When Memories
Come Flooding Back

I watched the reports on the TV screen as Hurricane Harvey made its landing in Texas, causing epic flooding and damage to many areas in that state recently. Soon after, Hurricane Irma set its sights on Florida and the rains and the wind wreaked havoc in that state too. Because of wise preparation, communication and evacuation notices, the loss of life was kept to a minimum. Any loss of life is a tragedy.

What really struck me was the heroism of ordinary people. It exemplifies the very best of our human nature. Those images of neighbor helping neighbor, complete strangers risking their own lives to rescue as many people as they could and the many volunteers from all over the country coming to help in whatever way was most needed at the time.

It always awakens in me the vivid memories of my own personal experience in dealing with Hurricane Connie in August, 1955. My stepfather, mother, younger sister and I were spending the summer in a cottage by the Delaware River, in a small village in Pennsylvania. At that time, there were no ongoing warnings of impending bad weather and no cellphones. It had rained constantly all week. Six teenagers, including me, piled into a car one evening and headed to the local movie theatre about ten miles away.

By the time we left the movie theatre, it was dark and the roads were beginning to flood. We tried to make it back to the village but a sign warned us the river road was closed. The driver of the car headed for his parent's home in the opposite direction. We sat silent, filled with fear, as he drove through fast moving water up to the hubcaps. All of us were so grateful to this family for taking us in that awful, endless night.

We continued to be desperate to get back to the village. The next day we convinced one of the family members to drive us to the river road. We made the decision to walk the five miles back to the village. We could see the Delaware River was dirty brown, rushing by, still higher than normal. We saw parts of cars, houses and even a piano moving rapidly downstream. It was an awful sight to behold. I will never forget also seeing a frightened family on a makeshift raft barreling down the still swollen river.

At one point in our five mile trek, we had to slog through the thick mud of a pig farm. Some frantic pigs came out of nowhere and began to chase us. We took off as fast as we could in the thick mud. One girl lost her shoe but dared not stop to find it. We continued walking for quite a while until we finally headed down the hill to the village.

My parents and my ten year old sister survived a very frightening and dangerous night filled with added fear about where and how I was doing. Reconnecting with my family when we got back was pure joy. The cottage had suffered some damage and there was no power or electricity. Funny, how all that matters less when you have experienced the separation from loved ones in a storm and now you are all together again.

Gardens, Butterflies and Hummers

❧

Gardens are wonderful natural healers. Time spent in quiet observation there provides every visitor the opportunity to leave with a renewed sense of wonder and lightness of being. Even the weariest of souls can lay their burdens down to rest for awhile. Nature teems with incredible color and variety in a garden. The flowers and birds look so delicate yet there is a hardiness about them that is quite impressive. Each of them is a story of amazing survival.

Long before I knew any of the statistics or informational descriptions of flowers, birds and butterflies, I was drawn to nature. As a young child, growing up in an urban environment, my mother's tiny backyard garden was a source of fascination and delight. The early spring groundbreaking of the crocus, through dirt, pebbles, and sometimes snow, was amazing. Observing the tiny buds on flowers opening into a colorful array of soft petals seemed like magic to my four years old eyes. Before I began kindergarten, my mother would often pack a lunch and take me to the nearby Botanical Gardens. In the

117

warmer weather, we were surrounded by leafy trees, flowering plants and birds chirping happily overhead. As we walked the many winding paths, before we sat to eat, butterflies would be flitting about, sometimes landing right on my arm. I was awe-struck by their delicate wings and intricate designs.

Hummingbirds, affectionately referred to by many as hum-mers were only beautiful pictures in a book. It was not until I was well into adulthood that I observed hummingbirds in their natural environment. They look so fragile yet the ruby throat-ed hummers who visit our feeder now may ultimately migrate more than 2,000 miles in a year. Some even cross the Gulf of Mexico nonstop, which is a 550 miles trip!

We have a feeder outside our sunroom window. It has five test tubes, each with a red rubber stopper. It is totally mesmeriz-ing to watch the hummers insert their long, thin beaks into the holes of the stoppers and suck the liquid food, wings in mo-tion the whole time. As I continued my search for information about these little birds, I discovered that more than 160 types of plants depend on hummingbirds exclusively, for pollination, a prime example of the interconnectedness of all life.

Years ago, when I was working as a visiting nurse, in a city in Massachusetts, I visited Alice, a woman who had terminal cancer. She lived in a small apartment, by herself, in a large housing project. She spoke of many things during our visits including her love of gardens. She knew it was close to the time when she would not be going out, so she showed me the garden she had created for herself in her tiny bedroom. It was like walking into another world with small colorful, flowering plants placed in various parts of the room, at different levels.

With the sweetest of smiles, she said: Now I will be able to spend time in a garden for the rest of my days. Flowers are my dear friends who wipe away my tears and bring a smile to my face every day.

Consider putting the brakes on the hustle and bustle in your own life and visiting a garden, maybe even your own garden. Take the time to rediscover what my insightful patient, Alice, already knew.

Forgiveness

*Hatred does more damage to the vessel
it is contained in, than the vessel it is directed at.*
Chinese Proverb

As I was walking through several department stores recently, I noticed they were already decorated for the holidays. Thanksgiving Day was still many weeks away but here we were moving rapidly into one of the busiest shopping periods of the year. It prompted me to think about a different kind of gift. This kind of gift would have profound importance, such as forgiveness, but no monetary value. I have always enjoyed giving and receiving material gifts. However, I think it is worthwhile to consider other types of gift giving as well.

You can't purchase forgiveness. It is one of the most valuable yet difficult gifts to give to someone. It touches our sense of justice, our sense of right and wrong. In addition, it involves our emotions, including anger and resentment. Such deep passions of the heart do not always pay attention to the rational counsel from the head, even wise ones. Our revered Vermont poet, Robert Frost, once wrote: To be social, is to be forgiving.

Forgiveness is not a formula or a technique. It really is a matter of the heart. It goes to the very core of what we truly believe and feel regarding our interactions with others. Have you ever needed forgiveness in your own life? Was it given or withheld? If it was freely given by another, how did you receive it? If it was withheld, how did that make you feel? Answering these questions is an important first step in understanding how a person might handle the position of being on the forgiving end of an interaction.

Forgiveness is not forgetting or condoning. It is not an unequivocal decision. It is a process that takes time and plenty of self reflection. It requires a candid inventory of our many strong emotions and the pain those emotions cause us. Hopefully, we can eventually move in the direction of releasing that pain and reclaiming control of our lives. As a person experiences emotional healing, the capacity to forgive grows. When you gain a more accurate understanding of what forgiveness genuinely is and is not, that information helps pave the way for real healing.

I have lived long enough to have experienced both sides of the gift of forgiveness, in the giving and the receiving. The unique quality of forgiveness is that it can be a gift, not only for the recipient, but to the giver as well. Professionally, I had the privilege of working with individuals, couples and families as they made their own painful trip from red hot emotions to personal healing and forgiveness. Once the heaviness of those strong emotions was finally released, clients often spoke of feeling lighter. In many ways, they were indeed.

This holiday season what nonmaterial gift might you consider giving another?

The Journey
Forward

The Rusty Years

*It's not how you start that matters.
It's how you finish.
I don't know how I'll finish.
I just know I'll be trying.
Liza Minelli*

Growing older, beyond the age of sixty-five, has obvious challenges and pluses too. An active sense of humor is a must for the journey. In a recent conversation with a daughter in law's mother, I laughed, knowingly, at her description of the aging process. With a twinkle in her eye, she said: It is the rusty years that no longer come with long term warranties.

After the age of sixty-five, you become part of what I call the dash generation. That is the category you are placed in on most forms. You could be 100 and you would be categorized with everyone over sixty-five! Well, we may be the dash generation on some forms, but according to the census bureau, we are also the fastest growing generation.

One of the perks of the 65 dash generation is the freebies. Recently, on a trip to Virginia to see a grandson play in a lacrosse game, tickets were on sale at the entrance. One look at my husband and I, and our son was told: Oh, there's no charge for seniors.

Go into any McDonald's and you will find groups of men gathered around the table drinking their free senior coffee. At our local McDonald's, one man walked from the other end of town to get his free morning coffee. He felt he got two for one, free morning exercise and his free coffee. Years ago, I suspect, many of those same men would be gathered at the local bar to chat and unwind after work.

One of the funniest stories a woman shared with me about the humorous challenges of growing older has me still chuckling. The husband and wife are in their seventies. One night the husband was having trouble getting to sleep. He got up, went into the bathroom, opened the medicine cabinet and took out a bottle of what he presumed was a sleep aid. He was about to pop the pill in his mouth when he decided to get his glasses, turned on the light, and checked the label on the bottle. Good thing he did because the label on the bottle he was holding read, Viagra!

When my mother was in her early eighties, she also had some vision issues and was glasses dependent. She told me one morning, she reached into her bathroom cabinet and grabbed what she thought was a bottle of deodorant. After spraying it liberally under each arm, she was struck by how unusually sticky it felt. She reached for her glasses and checked. Too late! She had sprayed hair spray under each arm.

Years ago, I was visiting a relative in her early seventies. She was a cleaning maniac even at seventy two. She had just finished waxing her large kitchen floor. She asked me to take a look at it because it looked strange to her. I asked her to show me what bottle she had used for the wax. She had neglected to put her glasses on before cleaning the floor. The floor had been waxed with furniture polish.

As we grow older, I think it is increasingly important to keep a sense of humor and remain willing to try new things. We are the dash generation born before laptops, iPhones, iPads, even TV's! Fear of appearing foolish should not prevent us from learning how to use some of the gadgets. As in my case, it may be a slow process but rewarding when you finally master it. Several months ago, a grandson called to let me know I had won an iPad! I had previously purchased five tickets from him in his fundraising effort for his lacrosse team. The box with the iPad sat for months in my closet. I was waiting for just the right moment to learn how to use it. People, in their rusty years, tend to take a little more time to get things done. Might need a little more oil in the engine to speed things up! I finally purchased the book: iPads for Dummies, Senior Version and took the plunge.

One of my favorite verses on aging says it all, Life's journey is not to arrive safely at the Grave in a well preserved body, but rather to skid in sideways totally worn out shouting,

WOW, what a Ride!

Now and Next

*The perfect age is somewhere
between old enough to know better
and too young to care
Anonymous*

Recently, I have been thinking a lot about the aging process across time.

This has not been driven, as you might expect, because of my own aging. It was inspired by the realization that in September 2011 my two oldest grandchildren will be headed for college. For me, it epitomizes that whole awesome reality called life. One day you are holding a tiny baby in your arms and welcoming a new generation to the family. In what seems like a blink of an eye, that grandchild is headed out the door as a young adult.

For the young, growing older is an exciting adventure. Proud parents watch, with delight, as their infant rolls over, sits up and takes those first baby steps. These are only a few of the many milestones most children experience. There is an initial fear of the unknown and then total joy in the accomplishment. Chapters are written in the book of their lives with the anticipation of many more chapters to come.

Then one day you realize there are more chapters that have already been completed in your life than there are ones left to experience.

You are retired from the life that once filled your days and years.

On a recent group tour trip to California, I was reminded how this impacts some people. During the first night, the tour director asked us to introduce ourselves. He noted we were on vacation and advised us to leave our career information back home. Most of us were retired yet many people could not resist defining themselves in terms of their careers.

Soon after I retired, I had another experience relevant to the life after the life you led before concept. My friend, a retired chairperson of an English Dept. at a local college, joined me in attending a writer's group that was meeting at a local bookstore. There were about twelve of us who attended that first meeting. During the introductions, my friend and I said that we were retired. Before either of us had a chance to tell more about ourselves, the leader turned to the next person. Apparently, the fact we were retired made us less interesting. She never asked what we were doing now or what we had done in the past. Whenever we find ourselves in a similar situation, we have decided to describe what we are doing now, in the present time, before we reveal we are retired.

Eighty-eight years old Norman Lear, the American TV writer and producer, was recently interviewed on television. He was the creator of many very successful character driven TV sit-coms in the seventies, All in the Family, Sanford & Son and others. The interviewer proceeded to focus on his past accomplishments. Norman Lear, in a most gracious way, steered him to the present and stated: I'm more occupied with the now and next. I want my life to matter every day.

Norman Lear was on to something significant. Though getting older has its unique challenges, it is also a gift, the gift of time. The clock may be ticking, but time has not run out on the plentiful opportunities that matter. It is important to continue to stay interested and connected to the world around us, to strive to learn new things, to contribute in some way. It doesn't have to be large and dramatic. One bed bound patient I cared for, in my community nursing years, wrote daily notes to residents at a local nursing home.

What might your Now and Next be?

Life in the Senior Lane

Remember, you don't stop laughing because you grow old.
You grow old because you stop laughing.
Michael Pritchard

As I stood at the open cabinet door wondering what I had come to get, that's when it hit me that I had entered the wonderful, wacky world of life in the senior lane. It is a shorter, narrower road filled with some very different challenges. Staying as physically active as you are able is an important part of growing older. However, I also think a sense of humor is a key ingredient to staying young at heart. The ability to laugh and smile at oneself frequently helps to maintain a healthy sense of lightheartedness and joy. A very physically infirm woman taught me that lesson from her wheelchair. You could not help but be drawn to her. She was so youthful in her outlook even as her body limited her physical activity more and more.

I remember the day, years ago, when my mother called to say, I have a senior moment to share with you which happened to me today. My mother always wore a lovely hat when she was going out. That was not uncommon in those days. She was rushing to get dressed to meet friends for breakfast at a local restaurant. She grabbed her newest hat and quickly put it on her head. My mother was in a hurry so she did not check in the mirror, as she usually did, before heading out the door. Mother's friends burst out laughing when she arrived at the restaurant. They quickly told her a large price tag was dangling from the back of the hat! We both burst out laughing over the phone.

There is a very funny story I came across on the internet recently. Two elderly women were eating in a restaurant one morning. Ethel noticed something funny about one of Mabel's ears. Mabel, she said, did you know you've got a suppository in your left ear? Mabel responded: I have a suppository in my ear? Then, she said: Ethel, I'm glad you saw this thing. Now I think I know where my hearing aid is.

Today a number of seniors use texting to stay connected with busy adult children and grandchildren near and far away. There are all sorts of abbreviations people can use when they text. I read this humorous take from Reader's Digest on possible abbreviations for texting seniors:

CBM: Covered By Medicare, FWB: Friend with Beta Blockers

LMDO: Laughing My Dentures Out, GGPBL: Got to Go, Pacemaker Battery Low

Those of us who have the privilege of living life in the senior lane will experience a variety of challenges but we do have the choice to face them with a light heart.

It's Never Too Late

It felt like I was saying a final farewell to an old and trusted friend as I walked into the Verizon store. I had begun to refer to my increasingly outdated flip phone as vintage. I made my first visit to the tech doctor as I called her, when my phone appeared to go dead. I wasn't ready to make the switch yet. The tech doctor worked her magic and got my phone working once again. It was only a matter of time, she told me, before I would definitely need to switch to a smartphone.

About a year later, my phone died again, and another tech doctor told me the battery had died. The only way to get a replacement was online through Amazon. I was still not ready to make the purchase of a new phone. I wanted to buy more time through the holidays that year before I had to face the purchase and adjustment to a new phone. That's just me, vintage, like my flip phone.

Many people today stand in line for hours just to purchase the lasted model every time one comes out on the market. However, it was clear this would be the year and the month I needed to switch to a smartphone. My vintage phone was on

132

life support and began to let me know in no uncertain terms. Now the text messages I received were incomplete sentences or total gibberish.

So as I walked into the store that day, I was more than ready to move forward. There were major adjustments for me in using a smartphone. I could no longer have the convenience of fitting the phone in my pants pocket. However, I must admit the many advantages proved to be fantastic. First of all, my text messages are all totally readable now, no more gibberish. There are so many apps that open a whole new world of convenience for me. I felt like a kid in a candy store and my grandchildren think I'm a notch cooler now with my iPhone8.

Technology has advanced so rapidly in my lifetime, I am still awestruck by all that is possible now. I think back to when I was a twelve year old child and our family had just purchased our first TV, a black and white, twelve inch screen. We all sat in delight watching it that evening. Oh yes, we've come a long way.

Beginnings and Endings

Watching the hummingbirds at our feeder these cool September days, I am reminded again the warmer, longer days of summer are ending. These birds will soon take flight to a warmer climate and will not return till late spring. The flight will be a long one. They frequent the feeder throughout the day, storing as much sugar water for the trip as these tiny birds can consume. They don't have to think about it, instinct just directs them to prepare.

On a greeting card I came across recently, there was a comment by the writer Mitch Albom. He was quoted as having said: All endings are also beginnings we just don't know it at the time. How frequently, in our lives, have we experienced the wisdom of those words? This awareness often is not apparent immediately. Some endings are filled with so much pain there is no room in our minds and hearts to even entertain the idea of a new beginning.

When I was twelve years old, my beloved father died suddenly, from a cerebral hemorrhage, at age forty six. The loss was devastating. The hole I felt in my heart was huge and the grieving was painful. As time passed, the acute feelings of sadness lessoned. The hole was slowly filled with cherished memories of the twelve years I did share with him.

Three years after my father's untimely death, my mother met a man who would become my stepfather a year later. Did he replace my biological father? No, never. However, I liked him and grew to love him for himself and a separate bond was developed between us. This created a new and very significant beginning for me. I would never have considered going to college except for my stepfather's enthusiastic encouragement. He believed strongly in the education of women, women developing their own line of credit and having a skill in the workplace. I am forever grateful for the many doors to my future my stepfather opened for me.

Some endings, like the changing of the seasons, give you time to prepare but many do not. You are faced with a sudden shift in the natural rhythm of your days. The ultimate challenge is how you will choose to deal both with it and beyond it. One size does not fit all. Some people ride the waves of change slowly but in a forward motion. Others fight desperately to cling to what once was but is no more.

Each person has within them a unique set of strengths to draw upon as they face the large and smaller changes that come their way through the years. The most valuable of all these strengths is one's attitude. It is the major coping skill that directs all our other actions, thoughts and emotions as we face a lifetime of endings and new beginnings.

A Journey of Years

I recently was on a mission to organize our basement for the second time. Although I had put scrapbooks together through the years, I still had several unopened boxes of photos stored away from our busy years and many moves.

My husband and I set up a long table. The boxes were emptied, one at a time, and I went on a trip through the past. The stacks of photos were grouped together in plastic bags with dates and locations. I turned the TV on to keep me company during my task but never heard a word of what was said. Eventually, I turned it off. It was fully engrossing to step back in time as I sifted through the bundles of photos.

The many faces of family and friends brought me back to the times when those photos were taken. It was a treasure trove of memories, revisiting those precious moments captured in each picture. I watched my children grow up again. In fact, I watched their eager parents grow up with them. There were births, graduations, marriages, losses of some cherished family and friends pictured in photos, and then the arrival of the next generation, grandchildren.

This time the task had a different goal. In the past, I would take recent photos and create another scrapbook. This time I had a different plan. Three smaller plastic storage boxes were set aside. Each box had the name of one of our three sons on it. Each box contains a photo legacy to pass along to each son and his family.

I experienced every emotion; laughter, knowing smiles, tears of both joy and sadness. There were the photos celebrating all the birthdays of our children all over again. I also came across the other special events a family experiences through those busy, early years.

I know in today's world, technology provides so many more options for taking and storing pictures It is fun to take photos of people in those unguarded moments when they are being themselves, not posing for the camera. I also enjoy photo-graphing animals, seashells and sand sculptures. It is fascinat-ing to come upon a sand sculpture created on a beach then left to disappear with the next incoming tide. It is my hope people will continue to have the opportunity to revisit photos taken through the years. When the time seems right, they can embark on their own unique journey down memory lane. Believe me, it's a trip worth taking!

Transitions

Life is full of periods of change and transitions from one period to the next. There are various markers along the way, such as births, graduations, new job, marriages, relocations and many more. Time passes, it seems so quickly, because people are so busy living it. There is a wise saying that speaks to this reality very well: Life is what happens to you when you are busy making other plans.

Recently, I find myself in that period of life when I am looking around and trying to figure out how to downsize within the confines of our home. In the past we have relocated nine times. However, I have always been a sentimental pack rat so I packed all the cards and letters from loved ones and friends and every book we owned with us to the next location. Now we have lived in this same area and home for many years so the task has begun but it is daunting, to be sure. I often end up rereading the cards and notes from loved ones and friends, several who have since died, and then releasing some of them to the recycle bin.

Copies of photos, through the years, that have been stored in our basement are now being sifted through and divided into three plastic containers. Each of our sons will soon receive one of the containers. Again, it is an opportunity for my husband and I to revisit years past and laugh and cry and enjoy the temporary step back in time. We are at that point in our lives when we delight in moving forward but also enjoy a brief journey, through the pictures, of when we were young parents with three active little boys.

For some young people this may sound like a depressing transition. It really isn't that way at all. It is an opportunity to revisit the past while living fully and happily in the present moment of a long life. It is a time in life to acknowledge all aspects of your history and lighten the load of belongings you have acquired over time. This allows you to be fully present to every wonderful moment of each day.

Every morning, after waking up, one of the first things I do is read this question pasted on my mirror: What is it you plan to do today with this one wild and precious life?

Mentors

*Some people come into our lives
and quickly go.
Some stay for a while
and leave footprints on our hearts,
and we are never, ever the same.*
--Flavia

The word mentor has been defined as a trusted counselor or guide, a wise, loyal advisor or coach. The first recorded mentor was a character in Homer's epic poem, The Odyssey. This character was given the role of teacher and overseer for the son of Odysseus. A mentor is usually older and more experienced. They are the first people we turn to for valuable sources of information, advice and support. Mentoring is used in a variety of settings for professional, personal or spiritual direction and guidance. It does not require any formal education except in professional settings.

I was changing pocketbooks the other day and pulled out a

card. It started me thinking about the power of mentors. On the card is taped an AA medallion which is given to recovering alcoholics when they reach certain points of time in their continued recovery. Among other things, the writer and recipient of the coin said: You believed enough in me to pursue recovery and treatment options when I initially resisted. I cannot adequately express my gratitude for this gift of life you have bestowed on me. I often read it and feel tremendous gratitude for the opportunity to provide guidance and support to a person facing a difficult and challenging moment in their own life.

A person I consider one of my most significant mentors came into my life when I was sixteen years old. My mother, after four years living as a widow, met and married my stepfather. He changed the course of my life when he encouraged me to go to college. No one in my family had ever graduated from college. I expressed a keen interest in the nursing field. He researched all the colleges which offered a combination of Nursing and Bachelor of Science degree. There were not many options for that type of major in the past, but he found them.

Who have been the mentors in your life? Did you ever take the time, in person or in writing, to thank them and let them know what a difference they made? Maybe there is still time to consider doing it. Another way to honor mentors, who have advised and supported you in the past, is to make yourself available to be one for someone else. It can be a kind of paying it forward.

Solicitation Overload

T he other day, I reached into our mail box and let out an uncontrollable groan. There were ten catalogs, nine from places I had never ordered from at all, and six charitable requests for donations. There was only one charity organization I had donated to and their letter thanked me but attached another immediate request for money! Daily, I find myself spending precious time removing our address from these multiple requests and delivering them to the recycle bin. To say I am on solicitation overload is putting it mildly. This is only the tip of the iceberg as there are also the email ads and the telephone calls at all hours of the day and evening.

I was curious just how many catalogs are mailed out to the general public in this supposedly paperless society. What I found, in my google search, was twelve billion catalogs were mailed in 2014. What was also revealing was that one billion dollars is spent per year on mail disposal as most junk mail is thrown away and contributes to the country's waste levels. A few states have taken steps to deal with this as a costly environmental concern.

In my continuing research on this topic, I found it fascinating to discover not all, but many consumers still like looking at catalogs. Some consumers were quoted as saying they get ideas from them. I also read retailers want to keep you still dreaming even if you are not buying. They consider catalogs a powerful tool in the retail marketing strategy. Retailers target their catalogs to the customers purchasing history.

However, I did find many people, like me, feeling increasingly frustrated with the number of catalogs and charitable requests arriving daily in their mailboxes. I laughed at one man's account of meeting the mail delivery person daily right near his recycle bin and immediately disposing of the junk mail in front of him.

In my internet travels on this topic, I came across another fascinating aspect regarding the world of charitable donations. Don't get me wrong. I appreciate the need for supporting organizations that are trying to financially assist worthy causes, both locally and beyond. The title of the article is: Tricks of the Charity Trade, Donors Unknowingly Pay to Receive More Solicitations. Often, solicitations come with address labels, note pads, greeting cards and magnets. All these letters are asking for a donation. What was revealing in this article was that a large portion of your donation will go to sending out these items to you again, as well as other potential donors. I have my own collection of address labels, note pads, magnets. Now they are all destroyed as they are received. What a waste. There is a site called Charity Navigator where you can find out just how your potential donation is used overall. Then you can decide to donate where most, if not all the money raised, is used for the purpose it states it supports.

I had to laugh as I went through the usual ritual yesterday of tearing off our address labels from several catalogs. The first one was a ladies lingerie company definitely geared toward the twenty something age group. I left my twenties years ago. The next catalog was all about dog products. We have not had a dog in over thirty years. Any products we do purchase as gifts for dog owners come from the local pet stores. I happily dropped all the unsolicited arrivals in the recycle bin once again.

Against All Odds

*Two prisoners looked out
from behind their prison bars.
One saw mud, the other stars.
Author Unknown*

I have always been drawn to stories about people who manage to overcome overwhelming obstacles, whether physical, emotional or both. What has both inspired and fascinated me are the individuals who maintain a positive attitude even through the most trying times in their lives. They not only find a way to survive but thrive and lead full lives. As a young child reading stories about them taught me a lot which helped form the adult I would choose to become. I also drew on the role models of relatives within my own family.

As a former fan of the TV series, Spin City, I was saddened when Michael J. Fox, the star, revealed he had been diagnosed with Parkinson's. I just finished reading his second book, Always Looking Up, The Adventures of an Incurable Optimist. Michael and Christopher Reeve are my two favorite heroes.

145

Chris was the popular Superman in the movies before his accident. They had it all, but in the blink of an eye, appeared to lose it all. They each had a dramatic change in their physical status. With the burden of an apparently overwhelming loss, they went on to inspire us with their courage, humor and incredible resilience.

In the book, Michael states: I had to build a new life when I was already happy with the old one. How many times in our lives have we experienced some uninvited change and felt the same way? He goes on to describe: The answer had very little to do with protection and everything to do with perspective. The only unavailable choice was whether to have Parkinson's. Everything else was up to me.

Tal Ben Shahar, Ph.D., a respected Harvard lecturer and author of the book, Happier, Learn the Secrets to Joy and Lasting Fulfillment, states there is a genetic component to happiness. However, we all have the capacity to deal with our lives in a more positive and satisfying manner. He believes it depends basically on our state of mind, not our status or the state of our bank account. He poses the question: Do we view failure as a catastrophe or a learning opportunity? Opportunity is a hard sell when you are in the eye of your own personal storm but worth considering during your struggle.

It is not only the experiences of those in the spotlight that impress me with their earned optimistic approach to life but the people out of the limelight as well. Recently, I heard about two people who had lost their jobs. Though much of their days are given to actively looking for another job, they each found a way to cope by reaching out into their communities. The man, in his forties, volunteers some of his time at a local food shelf. The woman, in her thirties, gives some of her free hours to helping in a homeless shelter.

Pollyanna platitudes to deal with life's ups and downs have never worked for me. Real flesh and blood people faced with significant challenges in their lives and meeting them with gusto and grace, and plenty of tears and setbacks, they are the best guides of all.

The Granny Scam

Several months ago, in a distracted moment, I picked up the ringing telephone without first checking the caller ID. The young male voice on the other end of the line greeted me with the familiar name all my grandchildren call me. He also identified himself by name as my oldest grandson. He started a friendly conversation that quickly turned to a sad story and a quick need for money to be sent to him electronically. At this point, I replied this sounded like a scam and he immediately hung up. I couldn't help wonder how did the scammer know the name my grandchildren exclusively call me and the correct name of my grandson? It's unsettling to consider these days how easy our private information can be obtained from a variety of sources.

I have retold this story to several people and have heard back a similar experience either they had or another older member of their family. I have dubbed it the Granny Scam because those of us who are grandparents love our grandchildren and would be more than happy to help them in an emergency if we are able to do so. That's what the scammers are counting on. They seek out people they consider vulnerable such as a loving grandparent, a lonely or socially isolated individual or a person in distress after a disaster, or during tax season. Sometimes the scammers pose as representing relief organizations, or heating or electronic companies.

In a report from Reuters, one in eighteen older Americans fall victim to financial fraud or scams annually. Scams are not only extremely annoying but they cost Americans billions of dollars yearly. David Burnes, a gerontologist and professor at the University of Toronto in Canada, states: We're talking about millions of older adults each year and what's worse, it's very likely an underestimate. According to Professor Burnes, this estimate only counts seniors living on their own. It does not include seniors living in a facility. He also added that victims of scams tend to underreport the scams.

One of the suggestions in dealing with potential scammers is not to answer your phone if you do not recognize the number of the caller. Usually, if it is someone you know or wishes to reach you for a legitimate reason, they have the option to leave a message identifying who they are and why they are calling. You also have the time to check out any message that may seem suspicious. There was a message left on our home phone once from a woman stating she was from the IRS. She did not give her name nor state my husband's name but said there was a warrant out for his arrest and if he didn't call the number she gave immediately there would be IRS agents knocking on our door. We were aware of this scam so knew right away it was bogus.

There are several other practical ways of protecting yourself from would be scammers. Beside not answering the phone if you do not recognize the number, officials familiar with scammer techniques recommend never to hand over identifying information over the phone such as a credit card expiration date or security code if you did not initiate the call. They also suggest hanging up the phone immediately when a caller asks for private information or promises prize money in a foreign lottery.

So the next time your land line or cellphone rings, think twice.

The Reunion

Several weeks ago I received an email from one of my college classmates proposing a reunion but not at the college. The email had been sent to fourteen of us. There was a rather poignant message in the email stating: there won't be many opportunities left for us to gather together to remember and celebrate. I sat back in my chair and realized we had graduated in 1961, fifty five years ago. Her passing comment hit home.

Back when I was a newly minted freshman in a women's college in Rochester, New York, there were about twenty five of us in a class of about two hundred freshman. We were the nursing majors whose goal was to graduate in four years with a Bachelor of Science degree in Nursing. Freshman and senior years we would be on campus carrying very heavy course loads. The three summers and two years in between we would be traveling to various affiliations to function as student nurses at several medical facilities. A few girls dropped out of the program along the way. Twenty three of us remained and received our nursing caps at the end of our freshman year. We became a very close knit group. When we graduated, we were a merry band of just nineteen who scattered in various directions but kept contact through the years. Over time some or all of us made the trip to the college for several class reunions.

This year was different. We were that much older, hopefully wiser and wanted mostly to gather at a pleasant place to spend some real time focusing on just our small remaining group. The plan was hatched over several weeks of back and forth emails and a date and place was set for late October. It prompted me to pull from a shelf a scrapbook I had not looked at in several years. There were all those young faces staring back at me. As I turned each page, I stepped back to a time long gone but never forgotten. Mostly, I was laughing at some of our crazy antics captured in the photos. Then there were those times when the tears flowed seeing the laughter on the faces of the classmates who had died in the last few years.

At the time we entered college very few women, especially in Nursing, were given the choice or opportunity to obtain a college degree. When we graduated four years later, we were still a small minority of women with a college degree. Also, very few married women with children worked outside the home. In one of my jobs, you were not allowed to take sick time to tend to an ill child. Childcare as it exists today was very limited. In some professions, there were almost no women. So many wonderful advances have been made by women through the years. It is an honor to be associated with a class that faced so many challenges back then and dealt with them with courage and good humor. Now we will join together not just to celebrate our particular shared journey but all the changes that have occurred through the years to provide women so many opportunities.

Beyond Resilience

I must be willing to give up what I am
to become what I must be.
Albert Einstein

People who experience a traumatic event in their lives have a variety of reactions to the event. One such reaction is repeatedly reliving the initial trauma, in vivid detail, including the intense feelings they had initially. It is referred to as Post Traumatic Stress Disorder, PTSD. Most military personnel prefer to view it as Post Traumatic Stress, PTS.

Recently, I have been reading about another aspect of the reaction and recovery of those who have suffered a traumatic event or series of events in their lives. It was coined as Post Traumatic Growth, PTG, by two researchers, Richard Tedeschi and Lawrence Calhoun, who have written extensively on the topic. They describe how it is not the event itself but the struggles people go through that can ultimately lead them to experience PTG. They are quick to add the emphasis they have on growth is not an attempt to minimize the pain and suffering people deal with after trauma, which is normal. They also do not dismiss the possibility of dealing with PTSD at the same time you are moving in the direction of the growth they describe in their research.

Initially, it was unclear to me what the difference was between resilience and PTG. According to Webster's dictionary, resilience is defined as the ability to recover from or adjust more readily to misfortune and change. PTG goes beyond just survival and has a transformational aspect to it. People who achieve PTG describe a closer and stronger intimacy with family and friends. They have discovered they have strengths they were never aware of before the crisis brought them to the forefront. There is a much deeper feeling of gratefulness. Surviving the trauma gave them a different perspective on life and the chance to become more aware of new opportunities. It doesn't happen in a week, month or a year but gradually, people describe feeling changed or improved in a number of ways. Victims of trauma can attest to all these transformational feelings which the researchers now refer to as Post Traumatic Growth.

In my own life, I believe I experienced PTG. I was twelve years old and my father was forty five. We were watching our small black and white TV and laughing at some of the antics on the screen. Without warning, my father felt a tingling down his arm and a general weakness. My mother encouraged him to lie down and called the doctor. By the time the doctor arrived my father's left side was numb and his speech slurred. Three hours later he was dead of a cerebral hemorrhage. I was overwhelmed with feelings of profound loss and pain, tears streaming down my face. I struggled for months after his death. I kept going over the details of the day he died and the deep sadness

I felt. At the same time, I kept looking out the front window, hoping to see him come walking home from work at the usual time. This whole experience altered my view of life in very significant ways. Ultimately, what that process, PTG, created in me was a heightened sense of the daily importance of the moment and the people I love. I never leave home without giving a hug and a kiss to the family members who are there.

The research in PTG is still in its infancy but the findings are filled with hope.

Nature as Healer

The sun was barely peeking above the horizon as I stepped onto the smooth, warm sand of a Florida beach. You could see a few pelicans flying at the edge of the waves, looking for their first catch of the day. The rhythmic sound of the surf was music to my ears. I have always loved the ocean and the opportunity to walk the beach at dawn.

Nature, in all its forms, can bring us back to wholeness by providing an insightful perspective to our own individual, day to day lives. It clarifies whatever we are facing so the bigger picture emerges. Every season of the year offers spectacular opportunities for healing and growth. Pondering the timeless changing of the seasons can provide meaning and comfort through the seasons of our own lives.

As a young child, I spent my summers in Connecticut, free to wander the beaches looking for shells and swim in the salty waters of the Long Island sound. For this city kid from Brooklyn, New York, it was pure heaven. The swimming required an adult accompany me. The shell hunting, in the wee hours of each new day, I did alone. To get to one favorite beach I had to walk a dirt path surrounded by tall grasses. I felt like I was embarking on some great secret adventure to my own private beach! The sand was coarse to touch but the beach was a treasure trove of shells. I would pick up the large conch shells and listen to the roar of the ocean echo from it chambers. I often sang songs as I walked along the shore. The ebb and flow of the tides left a generous supply of new shells to choose from each morning. Nature is always so giving.

Have you ever had the joy of walking on a beach in the rain? One sweet memory comes to mind of embarking on a walk with my son, Kevin. His infant son, Devin, was asleep in the beach buggy. We had walked quite a distance before a gentle, warm rain began to fall. The cover on the buggy protected our precious sleeping babe. Before long, my son and I were soaked to the skin but kept the same pace walking, talking and laughing as the raindrops became a major summer shower. If you ever have the chance, take a walk on a beach. Let yourself look, listen, feel and touch.

About the Author

Ellie Bushweller graduated from Nazareth College in 1961, with a BS in Nursing. In 1987, she earned an MS in Counseling from the University of Vermont. She has published in several magazines; RN, Nursing 84, Maternal Child Nursing, Professional

Nurses Quarterly, EAP Digest, Cats Magazine. The Tree With A Hundred Hands, a children's book, with illustrations by Sally Markey, was published by Ellie in 2008. The Realistic Optimist, Ellie's monthly column, was published in The Other Paper, South Burlington, Vermont, for ten years.

Ellie lives with her husband in Vermont and has three grown sons and eight grandchildren.

CPSIA information can be obtained
at www.ICGtesting.com
Printed in the USA
LVHW080307220220
647895LV00035B/1194